SOMERSET

A Play-for-the-Page in Verse

THE CHARACTERS IN THE PLAY

SOMERSET, the Lord Protector of England

PAGET, Somerset's chief advisor

THOMAS SEYMOUR, BARON OF SUDELEY, Somerset's brother

WARWICK

ARUNDEL
WRIOTHESLEY, the lord chancellor

Privy-Councillors

THOMAS SMITH

LORD GREY

SIR RICHARD RICH, a lawyer

CATHERINE PARR, Henry VIII's widow

KING EDWARD VI, Henry VIII's son

SIR JOHN CHEKE, King Edward VI's tutor

YOUNG WARWICK, Warwick's son

YOUNG SOMERSET, Somerset's son

Servants and messengers

PART ONE

The play begins in January, 1547.

1: *In a dark corridor outside King Henry VIII's private rooms in Whitehall Palace.*

SOMERSET

Have you been in to see the King?
I went to whisper in his ear
But I was told he didn't hear
His choirboys when they came to sing
The Mass, so I just kissed his ring—
He didn't even blink. I fear
The state he's in is that severe,
He can't respond to anything.
The moment I walked in his cell,
A horrid, nauseating smell
Immediately struck me: death
And foul decay. I held my breath
Until I felt my face turn red.
It won't be long before he's dead.

PAGET

I'm sad to say Your Grace is right.
When I first saw him lying there,
So distant yet so full of care,
It gave me such an awful fright
The muscles in my throat clenched tight.
I tearfully pulled up a chair
And whimpered my way through a prayer.
He's all but given up the fight.
Though maybe it is for the best
That he will soon be laid to rest.
His health has long been on the wane.
If someone's suffered constant pain
And death's provided their relief,
It shouldn't be a cause for grief.

SOMERSET
The King's physicians still pretend
His Majesty will be okay.
While I was in his chamber, they
Were making up a pungent blend
Of herbs in order to extend
His agony another day.
They are too terrified to say
There is no lotion which can mend
A body twice its normal size.
They've been preparing to incise
A massive ulcer on his thigh
As well. They know the King will die,
But they will do it all the same
So no-one can say they're to blame—

PAGET
…When Henry finally let's go:
It is an absolute disgrace.
I quite agree that they are base
Villains. They scuttle to and fro
Like spiders, putting on a show
Of grinding lavender and mace,
Rubbing their oils into his face
And his limp hands to let us know
That they are doing all they can.
If Henry were a nobleman
Or country squire, and not the King,
The fools would do the decent thing
And let him peacefully depart.
Some people seem to have no heart.

Alas, there's nothing we can do.
As God is merciful, I'm sure
That it will not be long before
King Henry's suffering is through.
He'll only have, at most, a few
Cruel days of torment to endure
And then his pain will be no more—
You'll tell me if I'm keeping you,
Your Grace? I'd hate to think that I'm
Causing you to run late. Your time
Is precious. I myself have much
To do this evening. It makes such
A lot of work, this sort of thing-
I mean, the passing of a King.

SOMERSET
You are the man to handle it.
It's times like these you come into
Your own. If you have work to do,
Then I won't keep you— I'll admit
I actually feel a bit
Overawed standing next to you.
I am not joking. It is true.
You're clever, Paget. You have wit
And you apply it to your work.
You're like a rock. You never shirk
Your duties. You just forge ahead
Tirelessly. When the King is dead,
I can't see any reason why
Your star should not rise very high.

PAGET
I'm flattered. I am somewhat thrown
By this. Please pardon my surprise.
It's good to know you think I'm wise,
But that means nothing on its own.
As the young Prince can't rule alone,
A plethora of stars will rise
And quickly fall when Henry dies.
I am a servant to the throne
And that is what I will remain,
God willing, during Edward's reign.
Your Grace's words have warmed my heart,
But mine is just a walk-on part,
Perhaps with one short line of speech.
What I desire is out of reach.

SOMERSET
I trust you, so I'll show my hand.
Give me a sword or lance to wield,
Give me some armour and a shield,
Give me a fresh and eager band
Of lusty soldiers to command,
And I will rule the battle-field.
My foes invariably yield.
War's something that I understand.
Fighting hard battles is my sport.
But launching an attack at court,
With words in place of pikes and bills,
Demands a subtler set of skills,
And I am only too aware
I lack a certain savoir-faire.

As Edward's uncle, I'll contend
With my opponents from high ground,
But if they should perchance surround
Me, I will need a loyal friend:
A man I surely can depend
Upon to win the magnates round
Before the youthful Prince is crowned:
A wise lieutenant I can send
Into the mayhem of the fray
In order to make clear the way.
Whether you wish to help me in
My just and righteous quest to win
Control is up to you to choose.
But you should know, I never lose.

PAGET
Your Grace has put me on the spot.
I feel dazed. Must I answer now?
You'd really have me make my vow
This instant? I will need a lot
More time to think. I've simply got
To have more time. You must allow
Me to consider fully how
I could assist you. I cannot
Take such a leap of faith without
First thinking long and hard about
Our chances. If I've understood
You rightly, your lieutenant would
Have to subvert King Henry's will-
With words in place of pike and bill.

SOMERSET
Indeed, my friend, that's quite correct.
Allow me to spell out your mission.
When I announce my new position
As Lord Protector, I suspect
Some councillors may well object.
You'll argue them into submission
And bring my campaign to fruition.
It will be tricky, I expect.
Some of them like me; some do not.
Some may accuse us of a plot.
I do not doubt that we will be
The subject of much jealousy.
But you will wear an inward smile,
As I will make it worth your while.

If you are equal to the test
And break the council in as planned,
You'll be my second in command.
I'll favour you above the rest.
I'll grant your every last request.
You will have power, wealth and land.
You'll take your place at my right hand.
Whatever measures you suggest,
Whatever course you make it clear
That you would like to see me steer,
And all that your enlightened wit
Prevails upon you to submit
To me for my consideration,
Will find my instant commendation.

PAGET
I have been offered many deals
By various ambitious peers,
Especially in recent years.
But this one certainly appeals.
All I need do is grease the wheels,
Assuaging council's empty fears,
And we'll enjoy two fine careers.
We both have moderate ideals,
So I imagine we'll get on.
Strong government requires that one
Brave man steps forth to take the lead-
We are not acting out of greed.
You are of young Prince Edward's blood.
The plan admittedly sounds good.

SOMERSET
Then we'll conclude our discourse there.
Your colleagues will be sending scouts
To ascertain your whereabouts—
You said you've not much time to spare.
Moreover, it is only fair
I let you analyse your doubts
And study all the ins and outs
Before you choose to take a share
In governing our noble state.
For you, I am prepared to wait.
But do not keep me in suspense.
Come quickly to my residence
The moment you have aught to say,
No matter if it's night or day.

Listen! I hear King Henry groan…
He hasn't heard what we have said?
No, no. He's likely being bled.
The greatest King this land has known.
He must feel terribly alone,
Confined, imprisoned in his bed,
Fully aware he'll soon be dead,
And yet unable to bemoan
The slow eclipsing of his life.
Ah well, the world is full of strife.
When one man dies, another's born.
After the night, there follows dawn.
There's not much point in feeling sorrow.
Goodnight. I'll see you in the morrow.

2: *In the newly refurbished rooms of the former monastery, now belonging to Somerset, of Syon House in London.*

SOMERSET

Has any man, low-born or great,
Ever been able to depend
On such an honest, loyal friend?
You've laboured daily to create
The framework for my grand estate.
You've toiled towards a selfless end.
In gratitude I will extend
You every privilege that fate
Has fortunately granted me.
As leader and advisor we
Will rule this nation side by side.
I'll take you as my foremost guide.
Here, let me fill your cup with wine.
England, my friend, is yours and mine.

I have arranged a little treat.
My busy cooks have worked all day
To conjure up this fine array
Of golden pastries and spiced meat.
Here, let me show you to your seat.
It is a marvellous display.
It seems a pity, in a way,
That you and I will have to eat
Something so pleasing to the eye.
Art will be lost and man shall die,
Ey, Paget? But that's quite enough
Of all that contemplative stuff.
We are both here to celebrate.
What's mine is yours, so fill your plate.

PAGET

When I stepped through Your Grace's door,
You kindly led me by the hand
Into a new, fantastic land.
I've never looked on such a store
Of rich, indulgent food before.
The pastries do seem truly grand.
And I can say that, as I stand
Here now, I couldn't ask for more.
However, there is work to do.
I'm sorry to abandon you
And turn my back on all this food.
I'm only too aware how rude
This is of me but, even so,
I am afraid I have to go.

SOMERSET

My cooks have made all this for you.
Would you like something else to start?
If it's on any butcher's chart,
They'll cook it up and bring it through.
The table has been set for two,
For us, my friend. You can't depart.
Shall we attempt this dainty tart?
We've just pulled off a mighty coup.
Such is the vastness of my debt,
A thousand feasts could not offset
Even the smallest part of it.
I don't have any wish to sit
Here by myself, without my guest.
My appetite would be suppressed.

PAGET

I cannot eat a single bite.
Your Grace should know that when I pled
Our case to council in your stead,
I have to say that I caught sight
Of some hard faces that dark night.
Their reservations went unsaid.
However, I was filled with dread
That someone would put up a fight.
Of course, it all went through okay.
Heaven be thanked, we got our way.
They sanctioned the Protectorate.
But, staring at this empty plate,
I still can see that ring of faces
And in the middle is Your Grace's.

SOMERSET

You witnessed the release of pent
Up sorrow that the King has died
Which simply chanced to coincide
With your securing their consent
To back our mutual ascent
To power. They are on our side.
The fact not one of them denied
The new last will and testament
Proves they agree with us in full.
The old one was unworkable.
Of course they didn't start a fight.
The council knows that we are right.
You have to focus on the facts.
They like me, Paget, so relax.

PAGET

I'm sure the councillors all mourn
Our much-loved monarch's sad demise.
But I gazed deep into their eyes
And I feel duty-bound to warn
Your Grace that some of them felt torn
Over our present enterprise.
They smiled but they could not disguise
A momentary look of scorn
When they at first regarded me.
They're clearly stung by jealousy.
Bestowing titles, land and cash
Stopped there from being any clash.
They have accepted that we need
One strong and able chief to lead.

But greed begot this line of thought.
And if the councillors affect
Some outward signs of their respect,
Don't fool yourself, it has been bought.
Their fond embraces count for nought.
Your Grace might reasonably object
That people like you. Yes, correct.
I simply mean to say we ought
To realise that some will feign
Friendship and love for personal gain.
We always have to be aware
That, while our colleagues seem to care
About us, we have not yet won.
Rather, our job has just begun.

SOMERSET

A fine philosopher once said
That when the body politic
Shows the first signs of growing sick,
It must at once be coolly bled
Before the poison starts to spread.
If the physician isn't quick,
The tainted life-blood will run thick
And cause a clot inside the head.
It will choke off the Rule of Law
And there will be internal war.
The substance of the nation will
Rampage against itself until
There's nothing but a lifeless frame.
Paget, old friend, I need a name.

I'll always follow your advice.
I made a life-long pledge to you
And I intend to see it through.
So tell me now which vein to slice.
Advise me and I won't think twice.
It's a foul job to have to do,
But rest assured he'll get his due.
I'll make him pay the rightful price
For coveting the place that I,
The place that *we*, now occupy.
I'll make him give his lands away,
And I will force him to repay
The cash he joyfully received
When Henry died and England grieved.

PAGET

If I could give Your Grace a name,
Which I cannot, we would assuage
His fears, not fly into a rage.
There's no one councillor to blame
For querying Your Grace's claim
To, as it were, take centre stage
Until King Edward comes of age.
We can't reduce this to a game
Of red and blue, of good and bad.
I would imagine most are glad
That you're, in practice, head of state.
And you can set the doubters straight
By showing them you're not too proud
To take direction from the crowd.

Your Grace must obviously lead,
But show them that you won't dictate.
Prove to them all that you will wait
Until the council is agreed
Before you purpose to proceed
On any policy of state,
Whether or not it's light in weight.
Make it your boast that you'll concede
When you have faltered, and abide
By what the greater part decide.
I didn't mean to frighten you
And make you worry over who
This strange, invented enemy,
This phantom in the mist might be.

SOMERSET

Forget it, Paget. I don't scare.
You've stated some wise words today
In your own cautious, tactful way.
Such honesty is very rare.
I know your meaning, don't despair.
Old friendships mean you can't convey
What, otherwise, you'd freely say.
It wouldn't be polite or fair.
I understand and sympathise.
You won't reveal who's telling lies.
But that's enough of state affairs.
This wine will banish all our cares.
Tuck in before the meat goes dry.
You won't name names and nor will I.

3: *At the Palace of Westminster.*

SOMERSET
The miserable way you draw
Within yourself as I relate
The challenge posed to my estate
By the incumbent chancellor
Betrays your rudeness in the law.
Is his ability so great
Such as to keep you in this state
Of fawning deference and awe?
I favoured you above the rest.
I knew, *I thought*, you were the best.
I thought you wouldn't fail to see
A golden opportunity
When one should chance to come along.
Unfortunately, I was wrong.

Don't talk! Don't talk, Sir Richard, please!
I tire of looking at your wan
Face. Here, put on your coat. Be gone!
I cannot keep a man when he's
So evidently ill at ease.
See if you can't alight upon
The star, your senior colleague, one
Southwell. A man of expertise.
His chambers are at Lincoln's Inn.
You'll find him if you search therein.
I'm sure that he'll be able to
Resolve my little bind, aren't you?
I have him as a shoe-in for
The office of lord chancellor.

—I know entirely how you feel.
I know how trying it would be
To bear responsibility
Over the entire commonweal,
Alone employing the great seal
To check or sanction each decree
Made by no less a man than me.
You'd surely find it an ordeal.
Is that not so, Sir Richard Rich?
The job requires a metal which
Southwell has demonstrated in
Multiple cases. Lincoln's Inn.
That's where he'll be. Do not delay.
Tell him I'll meet with him today.

SIR RICHARD RICH
I beg Your Grace to hear me speak.
I've spent a lifetime at the bar.
I wouldn't say that I'm a star
But I believe that my technique
Is quite demonstrably not weak.
The client and the lawyer are
So often speaking from afar.
We're quite a funny little clique,
Us lawyers, but we like plain speech.
And, in that spirit, I beseech
Your Grace to state the case again.
I'll scribble down some notes and, when
I've thought about it, I won't shrink
From saying plainly what I think.

I do not know if you have fitted
The old fool up. I only know
That I, in court, will have to show,
Nay prove, what crime he has committed.
Before the case can be submitted,
And subsequently undergo
A full examination, blow
For blow, with prosecution pitted
Against defence, I must make sense-
Before, I say, it can commence-
Of what exactly is his crime.
I do not waste Your Grace's time.
Maybe I've spoken out of place,
But I have got to know the case.

SOMERSET
I have been angling for a sign
To prove that you are not as mild
As some vain men would have you styled.
You haven't overstepped the line.
I'll pour us both a cup of wine.
Although I feel a little riled
At being treated like a child,
You've shown me that you have a spine.
I need a lawyer with some grit.
I have one here, I'm sure of it.
I find there are too many men
Who chose to remain quiet when
They should speak up and have their say.
It is no use just giving way.

I will ignore the implication
That I am hiding my true aim,
Playing some kind of tricky game.
My sense of duty to the nation
Alone begets my allegation.
You nearly made a harmful claim,
Sir Richard. But it's all the same.
You were expressing your frustration
And my great rank within the state
Was rightly given little weight.
As I made clear, I had to see
That you are the right man for me.
And, as I said, you showed some grit,
Some guts, and there's an end to it.

I have no proof to speak of yet.
But if you can remember back
To when Wriothesley used the rack
On a young woman, a brunette,
And if you can still see her sweat
As the cruel beast takes up the slack,
Causing her brittle bones to crack,
You'll know the chancellor's a threat.
Our task is to unearth a slur
So native to his temper, were
He to deny the wretched act,
People would treat it as a fact
The more so for his gracing it
As a meet target for his wit.

It might prove useful to explore
Wriothesley's London residence.
After he's skirted round the fence
And used his weight to force the door,
A decent agent would be sure
To find a suitable offence.
And you'll be able to make sense
Of all the evidence before
The crime is even brought to light.
I'll see you've had the time to write
A lengthy and convincing script
Before Wriothesley has equipped
Himself with paper, pen and ink.
Now tell me, plainly, what you think.

SIR RICHARD RICH
Well, to speak plainly, I'm still here.
I am content that, if we must
Break in, in *this* case it is just.
My conscience is entirely clear.
But please, Your Grace, becalm my fear
That your suggestions aren't robust.
I desperately want to trust
That things are as they would appear
And hints of my advancement to
A certain office are all true.
But say again what I will be
Once the position is made free.
I cannot risk so much unless
Your Grace explicitly says 'yes'.

SOMERSET

When I have said a fond farewell
In soothing tones and held him near,
Seeming to groan and shed a tear
As he is shoved inside his cell,
I think- *I'm sure*- I can foretell
A new and dazzling career
Will come your way by late this year,
In which I'm sure you will excel.
Yes, you will take Wriothesley's place,
Provided that you win the case.
Like you, Wriothesley knows his art,
But you will have a good head start.
You will be given means and time.
All you must do is find the crime.

SIR RICHARD RICH

Your Grace has given me a taste,
More than a taste, of things to come.
But should my minister succumb
To nerves and work in too much haste,
And should some papers be misplaced-
The image makes my body numb-
What then, I wonder, will become
Of my career? I'd be disgraced.
The chancellor would trace it back
To me and *I'd* be on the rack.
I have been lucky in the law.
Becoming the next chancellor
Would be the icing on the cake.
But God! The chance that I must take.

If I could manage to recruit
An agent who was sure to heed
My every word it might succeed.
But who would follow such a suit?
It is my job to prosecute
Those who fall foul to wanton greed,
So far from sanctioning the deed
And paying out a wage to boot.
I simply don't know anyone
Whom I could trust and count upon.
The only agents I'm aware of
Are those whom I have taken care of.
A few are now at liberty
But they are none too fond of me.

SOMERSET
Aren't they? Then you must smear your face
And hide your features with black ink,
And you must soak your clothes in drink
To make a good disguise in case
You're seen outside Wriothesley's place.
Sir Richard, why have you turned pink?
This is a good solution, don't you think?
Don't worry, Rich. He will not trace
It back to you. Sit down, sit down.
You are a lawyer, not a clown.
It was a joke. I'll use my man.
You use your ink to write a plan-
That is a better use by far
Than blacking out your face. Ha ha!

4: *At Catherine Parr's dower manor in Chelsea.*

CATHERINE PARR
Initially I felt surprise.
Until King Henry's final day
I didn't think he'd pass away.
His waking hours weren't filled with sighs,
Nor the long nights with anguished cries.
Whenever someone knelt to pray
The King put on a brave display,
Summoning all his strength to rise.
Looking the fellow in the eye,
Henry would straightly ask him why
He chose to scuff and graze his knees
When he could rather be at ease
Sat in the corner on a chair-
Such was the King's defiant air.

I thought the funeral parade
Was so well-planned and dignified
That I, at last, broke down and cried.
To see the King, my husband, laid
Before the crowd while music played-
I questioned if he'd really died.
An awful fear rose deep inside.
I looked away until I made
Myself accept that he was gone.
A part of him, I know, lives on.
Edward will prove his father's son
When he is old enough to run
This grieving nation on his own.
He is a dear, and how he's grown!

I noticed at the coronation
There was a mood of great relief,
Confirming my long-held belief
That, in the younger generation,
We can find hope and consolation.
We can turn over a new leaf
And teach ourselves to cope with grief.
I think the young are our salvation;
So quick to question and conceive;
So willing, eager to believe.
And then the way that children smile,
Oblivious to all the guile
That makes a pupil of the teacher
And a false bigot of the preacher.

Your brother, I must say, has been
Extremely kind to me of late.
He told me there'd be no debate
That I am still to be styled *queen*.
It's very clear from what I've seen
That he is, even now, the great
And selfless servant of the state
That I'd expected and foreseen.
And he has not forgotten you,
If news of your new role is true.
Two brothers, ruling side by side.
You must be full of sibling pride.
I've always thought, if truth be told,
That you are both of the same mould.

THOMAS SEYMOUR, BARON OF SUDELEY

Lord Somerset, if truth be told,
Is rather different from me-
I fear it's all too plain to see,
Like many who are growing old,
My brother has filled out his mould,
Becoming more, quite literally,
Than I can ever hope to be.
Were a new servant to behold
Us both discoursing with each other,
He wouldn't guess the Duke's my brother.
I seriously wonder whether
I would connect us both together,
Were it not for our family name
Which is decidedly the same.

CATHERINE PARR

Thomas, you always make me smile.
It was so sad to look upon
The King and think that he is gone.
Although I am quite certain I'll
Miss him, it has been such a while
Since I have shared a union
Founded on love with anyone.
I wanted to walk down the aisle
And take his hand in mine and feel
That all the vows I made were real.
Perhaps they were. It's hard to say.
Time hasn't tampered with the day
When we broke off our courtship, though.
Thomas, how long was that ago?

THOMAS SEYMOUR, BARON OF SUDELEY

You are determined to frustrate
My efforts to relieve your pain.
Just what do you expect to gain
By hearing an old lover prate
About the harsh designs of fate?
Remembering that day again
Is like to drive us both insane.
I can't, *I won't* perpetuate
Your self-destructive disposition.
Consider that an admonition.
But really, in all earnestness,
I cannot bring it up unless
You are prepared to see me weep.
Some memories, my dear, run deep.

CATHERINE PARR

Forgive me, Thomas. If I'd known
That you're still battling despair,
I would have spoken with more care.
There have been times, I fully own,
When I myself was often prone
To sigh and weep that you weren't there.
Sometimes it all seemed so unfair.
I felt like I was all alone.
Henry would ride and hunt and fish,
And I would stay indoors and wish
That you would take me far away.
But women always find a way
To reconcile themselves to fate.
We manage: our defining trait.

THOMAS SEYMOUR, BARON OF SUDELEY

The fortitude with which you're blessed
Was all my happiness and cheer.
My sanction would have been severe
If you had faltered and confessed
The secret feelings you suppressed.
But I was never in much fear.
As we survived each lonely year,
I came to see it as a test,
A noble struggle to endure,
Conceived to make our love mature.
You, darling, had the hardest part
In this great saga of the heart.
My passion for you lay therein:
No hero, just a heroine.

Can't I now say that times have changed?
What if I held you close and swore
We needn't worry anymore?
Can't a small kiss now be exchanged
Between two lovers, long estranged?
I've kissed you many times before
And so it can't be premature.
Why can't our marriage be arranged?
I love you and I always will.
Time will forever more stand still.
We'll stay the same as we are now,
Together, and we won't allow
Ourselves to be controlled by fate.
Belief: an old romantic's trait.

CATHERINE PARR

Now you are being too absurd.
I'm sorry but I thought you said
The two of us can now be wed.
Suppose a servant overheard
All this and took you at your word.
Before we knew it, news would spread
That I am sleeping in your bed.
I do not think I've ever heard
Such idle talk in all my life.
The thought that I could be your wife-
As if my marriage to the King
Was just a silly little fling
Which no-one will bring up again.
It's *you* who'll drive us both insane.

In quite another world from ours,
In some obscure Utopia
Where all the native peoples are
Content to while away the hours
Dreamily weaving bands of flowers,
We would reach out so very far
As to pluck down the problem star.
True love would grant us special powers.
If you could take me to this place,
We'd live and love without disgrace.
But this is England. Edward cries
Over his father's sad demise.
Thomas, I can't become your bride
Until the *memory* has died.

THOMAS SEYMOUR, BARON OF SUDELEY
I'm sorry. It's a bad physician
Who labours to relieve the strain
And only adds to all the pain.
I will not worsen your condition
By making any repetition.
You will not hear of it again.
I have already gone insane,
Making a marriage proposition.
Opposing fate must surely be
A symptom of insanity.
Only a man who is deranged,
Mad, could believe that times have changed.
King Henry hasn't really gone.
I know his memory lives on.

CATHERINE PARR
Please, Thomas, don't apologise.
Never to me. You mustn't fret.
I don't want you to be upset.
There is no reason to chastise
Yourself. You are so very wise.
It cannot be, at least not yet.
But what you've said, I won't forget.
You've made me see that there's a prize
Awaiting me, awaiting *us*.
The future will be generous.
What past and present takes away,
The future will, in time, repay.
Give me two years to grieve, just two,
And then, my love, I'll be with you.

5: *In Somerset's private rooms at Greenwich Palace, where King Edward is keeping court.*

SOMERSET
I must needs ask for your discretion.
Come closer, Paget. Can you guess
What this is? This is nothing less
Than the lord chancellor's confession,
Just now come into my possession.
I'm told the writing lacks finesse
Because he was in some distress.
I've ascertained that this depression
In the hot candle-wax was pressed
In with a stamp which bears his crest.
I've also checked the signature
And, well, I won't say any more.
He's guilty of a shameful crime.
Here, browse it over. Take your time.

PAGET
I authorised a new commission
To take my place and oversee
Proceedings in the chancery
Without the councillors' permission...
When questioned over my position,
I said that I had aimed to free
My time up so that I would be
Able to further the transition
Of power from the sixteen men
Selected by King Henry when
He was still living to the Duke
Of Somerset who kindly took
Control with Paget by his side
When Henry tragically died.

SOMERSET
Rich has constructed a strong case
Against Wriothesley, but I feel
It would be rather an ordeal
For such a well-known man to face
His downfall in a public space.
I'd sooner cut a private deal.
If he surrenders the Great Seal
And stays at home in Ely Place
Then I will let the matter drop.
Of course, there'll be a fine on top.
It will be costlier than bail
But, if it keeps him out of jail,
I don't imagine he'll complain.
Besides, he'll make it back again.

PAGET
There's something I don't understand.
How was the court-case built before
The news had even reached your door,
Unless it's somehow been pre-planned?
Although I see Wriothesley's hand
In certain places, I am sure
That this is not his signature.
There's something deeply underhand
About this whole affair, Your Grace.
I'll go at once to Ely Place.
I'd like to know which idle fool
Decided to invent the rule
That we can't organise our time
Without it being called a crime.

Wriothesley's predecessor went
Out of his way to delegate
Work not pertaining to the state
And *he* did not face punishment.
Surely he set a precedent?
I'll mention it at any rate
And afterwards I will go straight
To Rich and ask him why he's bent
On ruining an honest man.
The devil always has a plan
And there's no devil like a lawyer.
I will discover his employer.
Sir Richard's case will soon be shaken,
Unless I'm very much mistaken.

SOMERSET
You're good at issuing advice.
In fact, I'd say that you're the best.
You're cleverer than all the rest.
The points you make are all precise.
Your arguments are trim, concise.
In careful statecraft you are blessed.
In crises you are self-possessed.
And you aren't touched by any vice.
But, in this instance, you are wrong.
Sir Richard's case is very strong.
Your efforts, noble though they are,
I fear won't get you very far,
And the best thing for you to do
Is to accept Sir Richard's view.

The issue has already been
Put to a full investigation.
And there's a store of information
That only Rich and I have seen.
There would be harmony between
Us if you knew the motivation
That underpins this accusation.
I cannot let you intervene
In something you don't understand.
Have you thought over what you stand
To gain by meddling in the law
To help a crooked chancellor?
The concept of a noble show
Of friendship died out long ago.

Now that Wriothesley has retired,
We must work quickly to protect
The vacant office from neglect.
Sir Richard has the skill required.
He has, in point of fact, enquired
About the job and I suspect
He would be willing to direct
His powers as may be desired.
We usually see eye to eye.
He's too belligerent to shy
Away from backing up his views.
However, I would rather choose
A man possessed of fortitude
Than someone easily subdued.

PAGET
I think Your Grace has just implied
You had some function in this plot.
I pray to God that you did not.
I fancied only the green-eyed
Say that you have a ruthless side.
I can't believe that you have got
It in you to devise this rot.
I hunger for you to confide
In me and put my mind at rest.
Is this supposed to be a test?
Rich wanted to be chancellor
And so he found a silly law
Which no-one knows about to rob
A decent person of his job.

SOMERSET
I'm well-aware it looks as though
Sir Richard Rich and I have played
A rotten game, but I'm afraid
That there are some things you don't know
And you have got to let it go.
I promise you I haven't made
An error, and I won't be swayed.
Future historians will show
I had the foresight and the vision
To make a difficult decision.
I know Wriothesley's been your friend
Since you were young but, in the end,
We can't allow our private feelings
To compromise our public dealings.

The time is quickly drawing near
When you and I must condescend
To act like statesmen and attend
The first real conclave of the year.
The councillors will want to hear
What policies we recommend.
And so, my very clever friend,
The reason why I asked you here
Was to prepare for this event.
Over the past few weeks, I've spent
Most of my free time thinking what
Would go down well and what would not.
And I have waited patiently
For something to jump out at me.

I racked my brains to think what law,
What presentation or what grand
Display would benefit this land.
After a lot of thought, I saw
The nugget I'd been searching for.
The thing I really understand
And sense is how to take command
Of soldiers and succeed in war.
I'm an old warrior at heart.
I'm not like you. I lack the art
And the imagination to
See statutory projects through.
But show me to a battle-zone
And then I come into my own.

How many Scottish rebels died,
How many thousand did we kill
During King Henry's reign and still
That stubborn nation won't abide
By any sanctions we've applied.
Henry felt strongly that, until
There's union, the Scottish will
Remain a thorn in England's side,
And I believe that he was right.
It's clear to me we have to fight.
Their misbehaving will increase
The longer we remain at peace.
Nothing but war can set us on
The steady road to union.

Now, my dear Paget, you belong
In council, in the thick of it.
I sound as though I'm chewing grit
And it's the singer, not the song,
That takes the audience along.
And, what is more, if *I* submit
The scheme, I'd probably omit
The details or get something wrong.
No Paget, you're the better choice.
They're spell-bound by a courtly voice.
To start with you must take the chair.
I know the councillors and they're
Far from unfriendly to our cause.
They are well-used to Scottish wars.

And don't forget to tell them straight
Away I hold their friendship dear.
They mustn't get the wrong idea
About my seeming to be late.
Explain that there's no need to wait
For me because you volunteer
Yourself to take my place and steer
The early course of the debate.
Delivery is everything
And merely rambling on won't bring
The council to endorse a plan
The way well-managed language can.
A military man can state
The facts but you, my friend, *orate*.

PAGET
It is the Lord Protector who
The councillors expect to see
Beginning the debate, not me.
I wonder what you'd have me do
When they're all asking after you.
It's my opinion that you'd be
Unwise to play the absentee.
Remember this is your debut.
Your rank will generate goodwill,
Any supposed lack of skill
In oratory notwithstanding.
It really isn't that demanding.
And even if your style is lacking,
A good proposal will get backing.

A better role for me to play
Is making sure you have things straight
Before you enter the debate.
I've no strong feelings either way
On Scotland, but I would just say
Some councillors would rather wait,
Considering the feeble state
The Treasury is in today.
I'm sure you do not want to hear
That we should shelve it for this year,
And I'm not saying that's my view.
All that I have to say is you,
As Lord Protector, must be seen
To strike around the golden mean.

SOMERSET
There's no point softening my line
Just for the sake of one or two
Old clowns who no-one listens to.
If they don't like it, that is fine,
But I won't alter my design.
And just supposing, Paget, you
Are on the money and a few
Of the recalcitrants combine
In opposition to my plan,
We're right back where we first began.
A well-wrought speech might save the day
And only you know what to say.
It seems the irony's complete:
You've talked yourself into defeat.

6: *At the Palace of Westminster.*

PAGET
May I begin please, gentlemen?
Some of you I don't know as yet
And some I'd struggle to forget—
Having been friends since way back when.
It's good to see you back again.
This country owes you all a debt.
It's been three months since council met
And much has come to pass since then.
I don't imagine anyone
Could have escaped these goings-on.
Those who slept through the whole duration
Of young King Edward's coronation
Might not be fully up-to-date,
But we'll press on at any rate.

We don't have many absentees
But, as per usual, they stress
Their pressing duty to redress
Local injustices and please
The peasantry with guarantees
Of better treatment. They express
At length their great unhappiness
At missing out on the disease,
Public rebukes and general strife
That goes along with city life—
Were I not eyeing these sweet treats
Of sugared almonds and cured meats
Which they've sent over to us here,
I'd question if they were sincere.

Although it is a tempting spread,
I fear we can't tuck in just yet
As we are missing Somerset.
Perhaps I should request some bread
And cheese to be brought up instead.
On second thoughts, we would regret
Such wastefulness. Will council let
Me chair this meeting in his stead?
If he appears, I will step down,
And relegate myself to clown.
He wouldn't want us to be waiting
When we could rather start debating.
My Lords and gentlemen, a toast:
To Somerset, our absent host.

WARWICK
…Our absent host! This wine is good.
If Somerset were here, he'd drain
His cup so many times, he'd sprain
His wrist. And, knowing him, he would
Drink the whole barrel, if he could.
When we were soldiers on campaign
In Scotland during Henry's reign,
It crusted in your mouth like mud;
Not like this; this goes down a treat.
Here, Paget, grab a chunk of meat.
He's come to value you of late,
And you are second in the state.
The matter's settled. Let's get on.
Do we know where Wriothesley's gone?

PAGET

I had intended to defer
Speaking about the inquisition
Which caused Wriothesley's deposition.
From what I'm able to infer,
Lord Chancellors cannot confer
The special rights of their position
On any person or commission
Unless, that is, they first refer
Their scheme to council for approval.
Now, a Lord Chancellor's removal
Can be appealed for and effected,
Quite legally, if he's suspected
Of something vaguely untoward
By acting on his own accord.

His Grace has chosen to relieve
Wriothesley of his rank and pension.
He'll pay a fine and face detention.
I'm told there will be no reprieve.
A few of you may well believe
That fact Wriothesley's intervention
Targeted an arcane convention
Shows he had nothing up his sleeve.
And if Wriothesley only meant
To do his job and circumvent
The tangle of bureaucracy,
Isn't it plain hypocrisy
To say he's guilty of a crime
When we do likewise all the time?

My legal days are far behind
Me now but let me say, in all
My time in court, I can't recall
The innocent were ever fined.
They certainly were not confined
To their own homes and forced to scrawl
A note to sanction their own fall.
But there it is. The experts find
Him guilty of a grave offence.
Apparently there's no defence.
It's my opinion that His Grace
Laments the chancellor's disgrace
And he will come to realise,
Sooner or later, it's all lies.

To fight his cause, what we can do,
Assuming you agree with me
That our old friend should be set free,
Is put across our point of view.
His Grace is answerable to you.
And if he's made aware that we,
The privy council, don't agree
That the malicious claims are true,
I'm confident that we will find
He's not too proud to change his mind.
The council has to be his guide.
As soon as council has supplied
The intellectual provision
He needs, he'll make the right decision.

ARUNDEL

If I may briefly interject…
Some of my colleagues at this feast
Tell me they *hope* he'll be released.
Although, whenever they reflect
On it more fully, they object
That council is a wounded beast-
Compared to what it was, at least.
But I am given to suspect
We only say that we are lame
To free our consciences from blame.
Stripping Wriothesley of his powers
Was not His Grace's fault, but ours,
As leadership without advice
Is nothing more than throwing dice.

PAGET

I have an inkling that His Grace
Will shortly be arriving here.
He truly holds your feelings dear
And it would not be out of place
If one of you brought up this case.
If we let evil forces steer
A good and honest man's career
Awry, who then could bear to face
His wife and infant son and smile
And stand and chatter for a while,
Knowing he could have put things straight,
Acted before it was too late,
While there remained both means and time
To prove there was no fault, no crime.

WARWICK
Lord Somerset will sort it out.
Don't worry, you two. I would bet
My life the chancellor will get
His job back. When I asked about
It, I just thought he had the gout,
Or else his humours were upset.
I'm friends with Thomas. He's no threat.
He'll be released. I've got no doubt,
No doubt at all. Refill my cup,
Paget and I will bring it up
Myself. In my view, it's the Scotch
Who we have really got to watch.
They are the ones who break the law.
If you ask me, we need a war.

PAGET
Well, you are not the only one
Among our military men
Who misses fighting in the glen.
His Grace would have already gone
If he could fit his armour on.
Joking aside, the question when
England will be at war again
Is pertinent to everyone.
The issue must be scrutinised
Before His Grace can be advised.
It *is* a question, I believe,
Of *when*, not *if*, we will achieve
Our aim of one united state,
But wouldn't it be best to wait?

THOMAS SMITH

Previous wars have clearly shown
That Scottish soldiers cannot wield
A pike nor parry with a shield.
They'd rather all be left alone.
And yet, despite the fact they're prone
To throw their weapons down and yield
To England on the battle-field,
The Scottish more than hold their own
In small-scale skirmishes and raids,
And they can also build blockades.
If we engage the Scots in battle,
I'm sure we'll slaughter them like cattle.
But conflicts which become defensive
Are always terribly expensive.

ARUNDEL

Like Paget, I am in no doubt
England and Scotland will unite,
But it won't happen overnight.
What worries me the most about
All this is if it did turn out
To be a long, protracted fight,
My colleague would perhaps be right.
This country's economic clout,
Alas, won't make the Scots withdraw
And it won't make us win the war.
And I think we will see that one,
Or two, or three, or four years on,
The unrelenting fiscal strain
Will cause the Treasury to drain.

WARWICK

Why don't you make it six or eight
Years? Plucking figures from the dark
Won't help us. Arundel's a clerk
And, true to type, he'd rather prate
On all night long than tell us straight.
A month is closer to the mark.
A month from when we disembark
We'll have them licked. There's no debate.
And we'll take seven weeks supply
Of victuals. I can't rely
On soggy oats to keep me going.
I'd end up spending more time throwing
Up than invading if I dine
On oats. I need red meat- and wine.

ARUNDEL

It sounds as though you've had your fill
Already. While my new vocation,
It's true, is just an application
Of the administrative quill,
I too have ordered men to kill.
Before I wrote my dissertation
Detailing council regulation,
I showed great military skill.
Commanders who have known success
Are not inclined to boast unless
They have to, but I will just say
That while you shun the courtly way
And still employ a martial tone
Of voice, my exploits are well-known.

PAGET

Perhaps it's time to take a break.
I'll tell the kitchen to provide
Something more filling, something fried.
Lord Warwick, how about a steak?
If we are lucky, they will bake
Some of those pies with quails inside.
Arundel, tell me, have you tried
Those small quail pastries that they make?
They usually position one
With all its downy feathers on
Right in the middle of the pie,
Ready to break the crust and fly
Away. Lord Arundel? Lord Grey
Then, you can have the final say.

GREY

I've my misgivings, Paget, but
I find they always disappear
When I cross over the frontier
And have to use my knife to cut
A Scottish thistle from my foot.
One thing, at least to me, is clear:
Our methods must be more severe.
There must not be a single hut
Left standing after we have left.
And don't chastise our men for theft;
Encourage them to steal again.
It's my belief that only when
Their rotting bodies feed the worms
Will Scottish rebels heed our terms.

PAGET
That wasn't really what I meant,
But thankyou very much, Lord Grey.
Given His Grace is still away,
And given also the extent
To which the views we represent
Differ, I think it's safe to say
That we will need more time to weigh
Each pro- and contra- argument
Before the factors all coalesce.
As chairman, I will now address
My dear old friend, Lord Arundel.
My Lord, please ring the service bell.
We need two small quail pies to dine
On and Lord Warwick needs his wine.

7: *In Somerset's private rooms at Greenwich Palace, where King Edward is keeping court.*

SOMERSET
How much did Warwick drink last night?
The Treasury cannot support
Councillors who drink wine for sport
In times when money is so tight.
I'll ask Lord Arundel to write
Me up a censuring report,
'Consumption in King Edward's court'.
I think Lord Warwick would delight
In reading that, tucked-up in bed.
Could you distinguish what he said
Before he left to Arundel?
Paget? Perhaps it's just as well.
It makes me laugh they've fallen out.
Do we know what it's all about?

PAGET
The subject for discussion turned
To war and Warwick beat his chest.
Lord Arundel was not impressed
That his opinions had been spurned
And so the meeting was adjourned
To let both parties have a rest.
Eventually, they suppressed
Their indignation and returned
Like naughty schoolboys to their seats.
Arundel nibbled the spiced meats,
While Warwick, noticing his wine
Had gone, decided to drink mine.
At last, in answer to my prayer,
Your Grace arrived and took the chair.

SOMERSET

It can't be easy to preside
Over a meeting when the two
People sat either side of you
Were made by nature to collide.
Although, you took it in your stride.
They didn't start their row anew.
I think we can ascribe it to
A simple case of wounded pride.
The meeting-room was nearly full.
It would have been a miracle
If nobody had been offended
Before our first real session ended.
The main thing is we can take heart
That we have made a solid start.

Of course, when Scotland was discussed
I wasn't actually there-
As you were only too aware.
But, knowing you, my friend, the thrust
Of our great vision was, I trust,
Communicated with real flair.
When we have union, I swear,
I'll make a sculptor carve your bust.
I'll put you high up on a shelf
And the mere mortals, like myself,
Will marvel at your features, pearled,
Renowned all over the known world.
And, underneath, I'll have it written:
Never by man was I so smitten.

Rows notwithstanding, let me tell
You that the council will comply
Will all our wishes, by and by.
The bottom line is you did well.
It's over and you mustn't dwell
On whether everyone saw eye
To eye. The council won't defy
Us now that you have cast your spell.
The case for union is sound.
Those who have yet to come around
Will hear your words rebound and chime
Inside their heads and, given time,
They'll outdo even Warwick in
Their zeal to fight the Scots and win.

Like you, my friend, I've always said
The outcome of a war is sealed
On paper, not the battle-field.
Many commanders have been led,
By reading authors long since dead,
To think that rustics tend to yield
At the first sight of sword and shield.
Correct or not, this view has bred
A dangerous complacency.
Setting aside our egos, we
Must ponder, in the next few days,
The details of the planning phase.
To get things moving and assist
You with this task, I've made a list…

The first point is we need to find
The best and quickest passage there.
Unless we plot the route with care,
We'll end up marching through fields lined
With trees and it'll be hard grind.
A well-constructed thoroughfare
That's in a state of good repair
And doesn't deviate and wind,
But rather links us like a spine
Straight through to Scotland, will do fine.
Moving provisions to and fro,
I happen to already know
From my rough estimates, would be
Far less expensive done by sea.

The second point we have to weigh
Is, if the Scottish do hold fast
When they detect the muffled blast
Of English trumpets far away,
How long can we afford to stay?
The conflict simply mustn't last,
Or our expenses will be vast.
The Treasury will have to pay
For transportation, wages, food…
Thanks to taxation, we've accrued
A modest store. However, there
Won't be a great deal left to spare
Once we are three or four weeks in.
I'd say we've got one month to win.

Anyway, Paget, take the list.
You're capable of reading it
Yourself. I've read you out a bit.
Whatever my poor brain has missed
Will not so easily resist
Your far more comprehensive wit.
Forgive my writing. I'll admit
It's awful, but you get the gist.
I never was much good at school.
It's much more fun to play the fool
Than writing Latin all day long.
If you think any of it's wrong,
Then take me as your pupil and
Correct it in your learned hand.

PAGET
Please, you must take this back and for
Your own sake, hide it somewhere you
And you alone have access to,
A safe, perhaps, or secret drawer.
Then find some papers on the law,
Out-dated papers, mind, to strew
On top and keep it out of view.
I will forget I ever saw
This list and you should do the same.
Take it! I'll hold it to a flame
And watch the embers rise up high
Into the fading evening sky
If you don't. Promise me you'll seal it
With wax and carefully conceal it.

SOMERSET
Of course, my friend. Of course I will…
I'm in a difficult position
Here, Paget but, with your permission,
May I inquire if you are ill?
Because, if you have caught a chill,
You know I'd lend you my physician.
He doesn't hold with superstition.
And I'm quite sure he would distil
A salve to sprinkle on your head
Tonight before you go to bed,
Mixed with some lavender perhaps,
To counteract this little lapse
In the smooth-running of your wit,
If that is what we're calling it.

PAGET
I think I must be ill, Your Grace.
Although, my health would be restored
If you took back your list and stored
It, as I've pleaded, in a place
Where it can bring us no disgrace.
I know you must be very bored.
But, if the council is ignored
And you jump on your steed and race
To Scotland, sword and flag in hand,
Do you not think they will demand
An explanation as to why
You chose to pass procedure by?
You know the council must debate
Before we start the plan, so wait.

SOMERSET
If we don't make a start, we might
As well forget the entire thing.
What good will waiting, dawdling bring?
The councillors will see the light.
Don't worry, it'll be alright.
We have already missed the spring
Because we lost our dear old King.
We have to plan. You know I'm right.
We're simply setting out our stall
So that we're ready. That is all.
No-one as yet, not even Lord
Warwick, is racing with a sword
And flag to Scotland. Keep my list
And read it, Paget. I insist.

8: *At Catherine Parr's dower manor in Chelsea.*

THOMAS SEYMOUR, BARON OF SUDELEY
Say that each night the heavens play
A little-known eternal game
In which the sun shares out its flame,
Giving each star a single ray,
So light and darkness, night and day,
Are different and yet the same,
And, in love's all-approving name,
You'll find me willing to give way.
Say almost anything to me
And, even if it's fantasy,
I'll gladly go along with you,
Believing every word is true.
But say that love has passed us by
And I will tell you that's a lie.

Only a lover tries to fence
With words the way a poet might.
We feel our stolen hearts take flight
And then we lunge and make defence
With verbal leaps of eloquence.
But it takes all our skill to fight
The rush of sparks that blinds our sight.
We're lucky if our suits make sense.
A lover's nothing but a fool,
Who forfeits all he's learnt at school
And leaves the ranks of normal men.
A lover's a strange specimen,
Created not by Him above
But by, and for, a woman's love.

We've talked about this once before,
But I will say it all anew.
I have no choice because it's true,
And I don't think I can ignore
These burning feelings any more.
I'm utterly in love with you.
Enlighten me, what must I do
To win you over and restore
That which we almost shared together?
I am not interested whether
The Duke of Somerset, my brother,
Construes my aim as something other
Than we both know it really is.
The choice is ours, my love, not his.

I'm not suggesting we should go
And make a public declaration
Of our engagement to the nation.
My brother doesn't have to know.
Why should he? I don't have to show
The priest a special dispensation
To take a wife above my station.
We are in love and we don't owe
The Lord Protector anything.
And, after all, he's not the King,
Despite the way that he behaves.
We're not his captives. We're not slaves.
We love each other, so why wait?
We must be brave and pick a date.

CATHERINE PARR

When beauty now seeks out my eye
In some exquisite work of art,
I lose myself and feel my heart
Completely captivated by
What all the strange motifs imply.
I stand and look at every part
And, slowly, bit by bit, I start
To sense intuitively why
Such wondrous, esoteric treasure
Can offer people so much pleasure.
Before you gave your love to me,
Beauty remained a mystery.
But now, at last, I understand.
Beauty and love go hand in hand.

But this foul city is a snare
To lovers who attempt to hide
Their feelings from the world outside.
It is a sorry fact that there
Are frauds and rascals everywhere,
Cowardly sneaks who, if they spied
Us both together, would take pride
In laying all our secrets bare.
One cannot step outside one's door
In murky London any more,
Unless one takes a servant to
Fend off the thieves who grab at you.
There's no such thing as privacy
For people such as you and me.

And, as yet, no-one can foresee
The future. The Protector might
Make waves in Scotland and unite
Us both within one polity.
We don't have any guarantee
That you will not be asked to fight.
I'll get a message in the night:
You won't be coming home to me.
Have I the courage to say 'yes'
To you, to love, to happiness
If, in the blinking of an eye,
I'll have to lip my last goodbye,
Feeling myself begin to fall,
Having first gained, then lost it all?

THOMAS SEYMOUR, BARON OF SUDELEY
Were the grim beast of war to rear
Its ugly, misbegotten head
After the two of us are wed,
It needn't give you cause to fear.
Whatever happens, I'll stay here.
King Edward's navy can be led
By Clinton acting in my stead.
You'd never wipe a single tear
From your sweet face on my account.
I can remember the amount
Of heartache caused when Henry died.
How could I take you as my bride
And gamble what we've waited for
By fighting in my brother's war?

It's striking that, whenever I
Am walking with him, people stare
And mutter to each other, *there*
Are the two brothers going by.
Some stand on wooden crates to try
To see us clearer and compare
Our features and the clothes we wear.
My entire life, I've wondered why
Everyone seems so keen to find
Some sign that we are of a kind.
For some strange reason I can't name
They want to think we're both the same.
They want to boast of how they saw
The Seymour brothers, men of war.

When I was young, I would behold
My brother showing off his tin-
Plate armour like a second skin.
I thought it made him look so bold.
He knew I liked it, so he told
Me with a cheeky, boyish grin
That if I overcame him in
A fight, he'd make me one from gold.
He was eleven, I was four,
And yet I threw him to the floor.
After I'd helped him to his feet,
I teased him over his defeat.
Of course, he chose to lose the fight
So I would think I was a knight.

I've fought in wars. What man has not?
The naïve child is ever keen.
But when the full-grown man has seen
A bank of oozing bodies blot
The sullied landscape as they rot,
His boyhood armour gives its sheen
To all the wreckage of the scene.
Each fallen soldier dabs a spot,
A dirty, bloody finger-mark,
On every panel so it's dark
With all the misery of war.
I did my duty, came and saw.
But when a soldier takes a wife,
Then does he learn to value life.

For all that, heaven only knows
What we will do if jealous spies
Attempt to cut us down to size.
If we're discovered, I suppose
We will just have to wear a pose
Of innocence and feign surprise,
Dismiss it as a pack of lies,
At least until I can impose
My will upon my doubting brother.
But trust me, one way or another,
We'll find the bliss we're searching for.
And not the ravages of war,
Far less the baying of a city,
Can lead a love like ours to pity.

There comes a time for everyone
When a great hope of colour traces
Around the mind's forgotten spaces,
Which, if it isn't seized upon,
Will softly pale until it's gone.
It's sad to see on people's faces
The proof that in too many cases
That colour all too briefly shone.
Some were too frightened, some too shy,
Some dared not meet with beauty's eye.
Can you imagine what we'd see?
What sublime tinctures, you and me?
It is our privilege to choose
To banish all of life's drab hues.

CATHERINE PARR
I know now that you'll never leave.
In my worst dreams, I could foresee
A time when you abandoned me.
But waking proves that dreams deceive.
The Fates have seen it fit to weave
Our lives into a unity.
Not long ago, I asked to be
Permitted a short time to grieve.
Although that term in not yet through,
I choose, my love, to marry you.
Do you not see? You've got your way!
We will be married, come what may.
Do you need someone to translate?
I'm telling you to name the date!

9: *At Greenwich Palace.*

SOMERSET
Miracles are your stock in trade,
The standard output of your brain.
You've done it, Paget, once again.
I knew you'd manage to persuade
The doubters that we should invade.
And no-one, *no-one*, dared complain.
Now, no more obstacles remain.
The plan not only has been made,
It has been sanctioned, signed and sealed.
I will be on the battle-field
In two or three weeks' time at most.
Your triumph will become the boast
Of many generations hence.
You've struck a blow for common sense.

The privy council's like a bear.
Inexpert handlers fear defeat
In every movement of its feet.
But grip the yoke with strength and care,
Return the beast's unyielding stare,
Refuse to countenance retreat,
And your control will be complete.
Pull out a fistful of its hair
And throw the fibres to the breeze.
You may do anything you please.
When all that muscle is made tame,
It surely will remain the same.
When brawn is broken, strength beguiled,
What then, except the name, is wild?

I can peek through the future's vale.
My mind uncurls and starts to gape.
The image of a war takes shape.
I see my army on the trail,
My bobbing navy has set sail.
And there I see my crimson cape,
Its graceful, curving, flowing drape,
Swishing about my coat of mail.
I'm standing on a mound or hill,
Informing Scotland of my will.
On noticing an English pike,
A native drops his rusted spike.
And, yes, my speech is being praised.
A bright, new flag is being raised.

PAGET
These are nice images, although
It sounds to me like self-deception—
I mean your picturesque conception
Of the unstable status quo.
For now the council is in tow.
They gave our plan a fair reception,
But with one notable exception:
Your brother said he will not go.
He was as plain and fixed as that.
Nay he responded in a flat,
Unmoved, uninterested voice.
I'll stay in London. That's my choice.
Our city-dwelling Admiral
Perhaps finds life at sea too dull.

After we'd had some wine and cheese
And settled down, I tried to find
Out something of his state of mind.
Has he sailed all the seven seas
And wearied of a saline breeze?
Or has the Kraken been unkind?
Some of my colleagues are inclined
To think he's trying to appease
A creditor of some description
By acting under his prescription.
One canny councillor suspects
A member of the fairer sex
Is ruling him, as like as not.
Myself, I think it is a plot.

Suppose he found himself alone.
Where would your brother travel to?
What conversations might ensue?
And what collection of unknown
Fomenters could be neatly sewn
Together by a magnate who
Is fiercely envious of you?
We cannot leave him on his own
To move unnoticed in this city.
You must establish a committee
With me as head and put him on it.
When war's declared and you have gone, it
Will go some way to ease my fear
If I have means to keep him near.

SOMERSET

You've gauged him justly, I regret.
I comprehend his ways as well
As anyone and I can tell
My brother is no woman's pet.
And if he found himself in debt,
He has rich assets he could sell.
You are not wrong. I too can smell
A plot in brew. He is a threat.
I've always known that, while we live,
We will remain competitive.
However it is very sad
When healthy rivalry turns bad.
He flatters me in loving tones,
But he is jealous to his bones.

My brother might at first appear
To be good-natured and genteel.
But once you have begun to peel
Away the bubbling veneer,
You'll notice something more austere.
His childlike, innocent appeal
Eventually looks unreal.
And, if you still should persevere,
You'll ultimately find a soul
As black and featureless as coal,
Impenetrable to God's light,
Better, it's true, kept out of sight.
It is an awful shame the way
Ambition leads a man astray.

An Admiral who stays on land
Is like a bird that spurns the sky-
My brother is a chicken, aye.
I have a mind to make him stand
Up to his ankles in wet sand
And watch his ships all sail on by.
I should solicit him to cry
The commonplaces of command
To his lost crews above the roar
Of waves collapsing on the shore.
Who does he think he is to say
No word of reason, but for *nay*?
Paget, you're absolutely sure
He chose to offer nothing more?

PAGET
He reached a loaf of crusty bread
And shakily tore off the cob.
He smothered it with one, large blob
Of runny, yellow cheese and said
That Clinton could take charge instead.
His temple then began to throb
As though he feared we were a mob.
His face became as white as lead,
Just like a man brought down by sorrow.
He chewed and forced himself to swallow.
With his mouth open, like a fish,
He seemed to make a silent wish,
But worry stole away the sound.
At last he looked at me and frowned.

SOMERSET
Well that's no good. If I'd been there
I would have questioned him straight out
What he was going on about.
If you decide to take the chair,
You must be strong, not laissez-faire.
He flashes you a fishy pout
And now we're thrown into grave doubt.
I told you council is a bear
And, picturesque or otherwise,
I've seen first-hand those lawless eyes.
You would do well to act like me.
I've never held with subtlety.
When I have journeyed north to fight,
Be sure to keep him in your sight.

—That admonition wasn't due.
My thoughts are all in disarray.
It's been a long and trying day.
It is my foolish brother who
Has earned a lecturing, not you.
Do we have anything to say
About the bloody-minded way
The French have all but threatened to
Besiege and repossess Boulogne?
Does the Exchequer have the coin
For wars in Scotland *and* in France?
It's my belief there's little chance
The French will try to take it back.
They are too spineless to attack.

PAGET

Whilst there exists the *aspiration*,
Deep-rooted in the Gallic court,
To call the signals in the port,
Most of the recent provocation
Was geared toward intimidation.
I've sent our promise to support
Those burrowed deep within our fort,
And I'll despatch a delegation
To greet the King of France in style
And cool his passions with a smile.
No doubt he'll issue some demands,
But it will stay in English hands.
Before I bid Your Grace goodnight,
Did you say we've a speech to write?

SOMERSET

We have indeed a speech to write
To help the Scottish leaders see
What an achievement it would be
Were our two countries to unite.
Ideally, we don't want to fight.
With any luck they will agree
To a sincerely-issued plea.
Of course, it mustn't sound too trite.
It must be honest, from the heart,
Diffusing very subtle art.
I can recall a pleasing line
Which strikes my mind as rather fine:
Two nations, one descent of blood.
Well, Paget, is it any good?

PAGET
It hits a certain kind of note.
I'm pleased you think it's rather fine.
It happens to be one of mine.
Before you leave, I will devote
Some time to fleshing out this quote.
I've scribbled many a rough line
Which I am sure I can refine.
It is important to promote,
As best we can, the crystal sense
That there is no real difference
Between our customs and our law
And so we needn't go to war.
We must provide them with a chance
To wake from their historic trance.

SOMERSET
We surely must. I might have guessed
So neat an abstract of our view
Could only have been penned by you.
My weary mind is now at rest
That France won't put us to the test,
And there is little left to do
Except to toast our latest coup.
However, you must keep abreast
Of all my brother's machinations.
I'm unafraid of foreign nations.
Whatever heathen land I stride,
I know that God walks by my side,
Conveying me through all my fights.
But it's the snake at home which bites.

10: *In King Edward's schoolroom at Greenwich Palace.*

KING EDWARD VI
Yes, *but*, my favourite Tutor Cheke,
How can I be expected to
Encompass all that Homer knew
If you're so hopelessly oblique?
Yes, I am finished. Please, do speak.
But, oh! The where… the when… the who…
Rhyme off until your face turns blue.
Why bother learning Ancient Greek?
Is it a pain? To what extent?
First plainly state your argument.
Set out your thesis, part by part.
And at the end, repeat the start.
Have I remembered your technique?
Ah, Tutor Cheke, you chew your cheek.

SIR JOHN CHEKE
Your Royal Highness is aware
That Homer was three weeks ago
And now we're learning Cicero.
And if Your Majesty would care
To cease from rocking on your chair,
Perhaps Your Majesty will show
Your giggling class-mates what we know
About the who, the why, the where
Of the last pagan century
While class decides if we agree.
Young Somerset, young Warwick, we
Will ponder whether we agree.
Young Somerset! Young Warwick! *We*
Means all of us and not just me.

KING EDWARD VI
Oh, Cheke! The class already knows
That stale old yarn. It hurts my brain.
We've done it time and time again.
Well, just for *you*… The story goes
When Ancient Rome was in the throes
Of evil, when the good were slain
And heroes called upon in vain,
Came Cicero and his great prose.
Not just a writer, Cheke, like you,
He'd lots of other talents too.
He was a pretty good all-rounder.
He caused his rivals' plans to flounder-
Until his luck ran out and he
Came up against Mark Antony.

That was a shame, but anyway,
Whenever Romans who were poor
Were made by tyrants to feel sore,
They'd get together and they'd say
That Cicero will save the day.
Some mornings there would be a score
Of people stood outside his door
And, even though they couldn't pay,
He would politely ask them in.
They knew they couldn't fail to win
If Cicero was on the case.
He never finished second place.
When things were looking pretty black,
Our dear old Tully had Rome's back.

SIR JOHN CHEKE
And did the suppliants who waited
Outside the great man's door and sued
For redress ever hear such crude
And grossly unsophisticated
Language as you have just created?
Your Majesty is far from rude
In rhetoric. I've made you shrewd.
Has all your eloquence vacated,
I wonder, to a sunny clime
And left me with this artless mime
For some street trader selling mead?
I think it must have done indeed.
One hopes at this point that you know
Why we are learning Cicero.

KING EDWARD VI
My dearest Cheke, if I displayed
A more befitting eloquence
In daily life from this point hence,
And if my theses were conveyed
Down a syntactical cascade,
Both intellectually intense
And also full of common sense,
You know I'd put you in the shade.
I'm reading Tully to cement
My grasp of ruling by consent,
And that whole axiom depends
On not embarrassing your friends.
And so, you see, I only speak
This way to save your blushes, Cheke.

YOUNG SOMERSET

There is some merit in this view.
The argument is good and bold,
The diction pleasing, well-controlled.
I think Your Majesty speaks true—
Cheke, he is cleverer than you.
For my part, I am eight years old
And I care not what I am told.
Therefore please see your story through,
Your Majesty, so-be-it crude.
My stories tend towards the lewd,
But crudity's the next best thing.
You are a very noble king,
And all your tales most excellent.
I feel our tutor must repent…

YOUNG WARWICK

…It seems we've struck our tutor dumb.
The King is right. He can't compete.
Cheke, fetch a cushion for my seat.
The wood is hard on my poor bum.
My *cheeks* are starting to go numb.
Also, I'd like a tasty treat.
If I don't have a bite to eat,
I shall be forced to suck my thumb.
I trust you, Tutor Cheke, to choose.
And, Tutor Cheke, please bring back news
Of progress in the Scottish war.
I felt quite anxious when I saw
Our household soldiers march away.
I hope my father is okay.

SIR JOHN CHEKE
Be quiet! *You— you little runt*!
If you believe I won't chastise—
Oh! Warwick! Come now, dry your eyes.
Your Majesty! You mustn't shunt
Young Warwick's desk. Please face the front.
Young Warwick, I apologise.
I told myself I wouldn't rise
To provocation. I was blunt.
I'm sorry. Let me dry your tears.
You're not the only one who fears
For loved-ones who have gone to fight.
But trust me, he will be alright.
Compose yourself. You needn't fret.
Your father is with Somerset.

They didn't leave that long ago.
They're probably in England still.
I promise, when there's news, I will
Immediately let you know.
And please, Your Majesty, although
I'm certain launching your friend's quill
Into the board requires great skill,
I'd rather students didn't throw
Lethal projectiles though the air.
I am not being too unfair,
I trust, in making that one rule.
I know that you are not at school
But, as your tutor, I expect
You all to show me some respect.

I don't believe that you should feel
Ashamed in any way to cry.
Only a bigot would deny
That conflict is a grim ordeal.
I don't expect you to conceal
Your worries, but you must all try
To be well-mannered and apply
Yourselves in lesson. The great wheel
Of time which splinters-out man's fate
Will, not so long from now, rotate
To put you in your loved-ones places.
When age retires, young blood replaces.
But now you're young, and youth's divine.
Your father, Warwick, will be fine.

KING EDWARD VI
Of course the drunkard will be fine.
If I were Tutor Cheke, I'd pound
Your empty head into the ground.
All that you do is whinge and whine.
No-one still cries when they are nine.
You'll see, he'll come home safe and sound.
You'll hear him staggering around
Trying to find a cup of wine
One night when everyone's in bed.
And he will reach the brine instead
And gulp it down indifferently.
And then he'll do a noisy wee,
So loud it wakes up half your staff.
And you'll lie wide awake and laugh.

As Cheke said, we should not forget
Who will be by your father's side
When Englishman and Scot collide:
The man with two great eyebrows set
Into his head like shards of jet:
The man who watches arrows glide
Towards him, dauntless, narrow-eyed:
My dear old Uncle Somerset.
It's sure to be a grand event
And I was happy when they went.
Part of me wants to join them there,
Leave London for the open air,
Make my late father proud of me.
But Latin classes it must be.

SIR JOHN CHEKE
Indeed, Your Majesty, it must.
I can recall the sheer dismay
When good King Henry passed away.
A soldier-king must needs be just
As well as physically robust.
It would be true enough to say
That there will shortly come the day
When the ambition you've discussed
Will be fulfilled. You wait and see.
The times dictate that when you three
Are fully-grown, you'll go and fight.
But, while there's some remaining light,
Before our keen, young minds turn woolly,
Let us return to *dear, old Tully*.

11: *The English camp at Inveresk, Scotland.*

WARWICK
I've moved my soldiers into place.
If you'll forgive me, I must take
A seat as all my muscles ache.
You'd think that we were giving chase
To fleeing Scots, the brutal pace
I set. I kept the men awake
All night. We marched without a break.
But here we are, on time, Your Grace.
My chiefs complained they'd burst a vein,
So unrelenting was the strain
Of those last miles through sodden clay.
We will recover in a day.
The men can't wait to get stuck in.
We are all itching to begin.

SOMERSET
I too arrived not long ago
And fell into that very chair
Without an ounce of strength to spare.
My progress was extremely slow.
We're growing old, my friend, although
At least our marching everywhere
And the untainted country air
Has given us a healthy glow.
As tired and old as we may be,
We're still two giants, you and me.
Two great, old soldiers on campaign,
Together, fighting once again.
Not much has changed except the wine,
Which actually is quite fine!

I wish you could have seen the way
The rustics panicked when we went
Straight through a native settlement.
The elders started to survey
Our numbers and then fell to pray.
The women wailed a death lament,
Perhaps supposing that we meant
To burn their hovels down and slay
Them then and there, like helpless sheep.
I've never witnessed young girls weep
Their fate so unbecomingly,
Spitting out oaths and threats at me.
These Scottish witches could outdo
Even the foulest English shrew.

Have you had chance to look around
For a good patch of raised-up land
On which to centre my command?
Through past adventures I have found
That he who holds the higher ground
Quite often has the upper hand.
I have been led to understand
There lies a wide and flat-topped mound
On the far side of the next glen.
When you feel satisfied your men
Have had sufficient time to rest,
Send out a party two miles west
With orders issued straight from me
To check its suitability.

The enemy is drawing near.
I do not entertain a doubt
That they will all have heard about
Our coming. Should we face them here,
We will be trapped like startled deer.
For sure they will have sent a scout
To guess our force and sniff us out.
They are advancing. That is clear.
I've put five thousand on the trail
A way out west to Annandale,
Which should have thrown them off the scent
And made them guess at our intent.
But time is something man can't borrow.
They will be with us by tomorrow.

WARWICK
I see exactly what you mean.
We are wide open, in plain sight.
Your Grace is absolutely right.
Their victory would be routine
If we remain hemmed-in between
These ledges. I will move tonight
And I'll be stationed by first light.
We're old, but better that than green.
We've found our weakness, so we'll move.
We don't have anything to prove.
The young discover to their cost
That if you're on bad ground, you've lost.
There's nothing wrong with being brave
Until it takes you to your grave.

SOMERSET
Unless committed to hold fast,
A general must keep his head
And look beyond the things he's read.
The era of fair-play has passed.
There is no gallant, knightly caste.
There's just the living and the dead.
Do not be brave. Be shrewd instead—
Can you believe we're here at last?
It's thanks to Paget, my dear friend.
He swung the council in the end.
Of course, I was convinced he would.
He is spectacularly good,
Superb at winning people round,
And all his thoughts are very sound.

WARWICK
I have not met the statesman more
Supremely talented than he
Is, I wholeheartedly agree.
But our dear friend did not secure
The Lords' consent, I can assure
Your Grace. He sat right next to me
And said that council mustn't be
Too keen and that he wasn't sure
The time was ripe to start a war.
If you had seen what we all saw,
You would now have some new perspectives
On Paget's personal objectives.
I do not mean he isn't loyal.
I just don't credit selfless toil.

But really it's your brother who
Is false. My liking for him cooled
That night when he would not be ruled.
I don't doubt people say to you
That I am just a drunk. It's true
I like a drink. But don't be fooled.
My eyes are open. Life has schooled
Me in men's ways. I can see through
The bows and nods into the heart.
I'm well aware that I'm not smart.
But I can tell what's going on.
Sudeley was glad to see us gone.
And if there is a poisoned limb
In England's body, it is him.

SOMERSET
Paget is perfectly benign.
Because a man's intelligent,
It doesn't follow that he's bent
On some vainglorious design.
Perhaps he spun the lords a line,
Or you just missed his argument.
You would have seen what Paget meant
If you had not been drunk on wine.
When I was ready to come up,
I'm told you emptied Paget's cup.
And when we left, you almost fell,
And then you blamed Lord Arundel.
For several days he was upset
About your slurred, aggressive threat.

My brother on the other hand
Finds commerce in the grossest lies
Conceived to charm and mesmerise.
Nobody would refuse command
Unless they'd something shady planned.
But do we think he's so unwise
As this outrageous act implies?
If there is one thing I can't stand,
It is a lack of certainty.
He's deadly envious of me.
But how far would my brother go
To see that little acorn grow?
I have confided this in you,
And now you share my burden too.

I won't allow my mind to stray.
We're deep within a hostile state.
My brother's stratagems can wait.
The task at hand is to convey
Our forces hence without delay,
Onto that field of eight by eight,
There to wage war, to check, to mate,
To form the pieces in the fray.
The pawns line up in rank and file
And gaze into the distance while
Competing wisdoms drive toward a
Solution, shrouded in disorder.
One strength of purpose butts against
Another. Battle has commenced.

Tomorrow we will build a pyre.
With hot, red faces we will dip
Our fearsome arrows by the tip
Into a ball of raging fire.
And as the molten bolts soar higher,
Causing the sky itself to rip,
The torn-up clouds will seem to drip
Bright orange for us to admire.
This prophecy of hell will arc
Inevitably to its mark.
The Scottish will be set alight,
Their bodies burn into the night.
If not as soldiers, they will please
Their pagan gods as effigies.

The arrows' heat upon their backs,
The cavalry will cut the planes
Into a network of crossed lanes;
Repelling desperate attacks
With sabre versus cumbrous axe
Or hammer; pumping on the reins
To meet whatever still remains
Sleep-walking over bloodied tracks
And slice it with an easy blade
Before returning from the raid,
Dismounting from the grunting steed
And gulping down a cup of mead,
Quite breathless from the exercise,
But with the flames still in their eyes.

Tomorrow England celebrates.
Tomorrow Scotland's living grieves.
The wizened chronicler perceives
Us from a distance and narrates
The foretold coupling of two states.
In several hundred ornate leaves,
With all the detail he conceives,
He scratches down the names and dates.
He writes a legend in which fact
And seeming fancy interact
To the great benefit of each,
To entertain and yet to teach,
To hail our deeds for all to see,
To win us immortality.

12: *In a street outside the Palace of Westminster.*

THOMAS SEYMOUR, BARON OF SUDELEY
My Lord Wriothesley, is that you,
Or do my eyes play tricks on me?
Are you at last at liberty?
It seems the whispered claims are true.
And let me say it's overdue.
What a great joy it is to see
Our deeply longed-for absentee
In good health, having made it through.
I trust you *are* in health, my friend.
It so, adjure that hateful trend
Of feigning gloomy melancholy.
Such fashionable stuff is folly
And altogether out of place
For one with such a happy face.

WRIOTHESLEY
I'm on my way to parliament.
I'm tired, I'm cold and I am ill.
There is a highly poisonous bill
Which I must struggle to prevent
From gaining general consent.
I must endeavour to distil
My views into a form which will
Convince the brainless country gent,
Or else it's going to succeed.
And it would seem that I must lead
The opposition on my own.
And now, God help me, *you* are thrown
Before me in this evil place.
Please cut, Lord Sudeley, to the chase.

THOMAS SEYMOUR, BARON OF SUDELEY
Oh, come now, that is not the way.
I'm sure the members will not fight
You when they see that you are right.
It's such a lovely day today.
There's not a single speck of grey
To rob the heavens of their light.
Tell me it's not a splendid sight
To watch the nodding bluebells sway
In such a cool, late summer breeze,
Watched over by the lofty trees
Which seem to utter, not in words
But in the merry tunes of birds,
The message that the world can wait,
Put off your errands and be late!

WRIOTHESLEY
Next you will call the sun a *jewel*.
I wish that I were still confined.
I must conclude that you've gone blind,
Or rather that you're just a fool.
Nature is cold and hard and cruel,
Unfortunately like mankind.
It offers me no peace of mind.
My colleagues are about to rule
On something of great salience
And I am late so get you hence.
Spend a few profitable hours
Considering your bending flowers.
And if you think of some quaint words,
Set them to music afterwards.

THOMAS SEYMOUR, BARON OF SUDELEY

Just one more moment. I'll be brief.
It makes me happy when I see
An upright, blameless man set free.
Indeed, it is a great relief.
It's always been my firm belief
A man who issues a decree
To take away the liberty
Of a good person is a thief.
Scouring the annals for a law
To ruin a fair chancellor
Was devious and underhand.
I simply cannot understand
What he was trying to achieve.
The charges were pure make-believe.

My brother riles me, I'll admit.
And it annoys me all the more
That someone who has such a store
Of knowledge, learning and sharp wit
Should lose his job by one man's writ.
When you were rudely shown the door,
More than a few of us were sore.
The privy council *can* acquit
You of this fabricated crime
And raise you up again, with time.
My brother is extremely proud,
Although, by rights, he's not allowed
To shake his fist and dominate
The entire structure of the state.

Of course, he *thinks* he is the King.
To speak with him, one first must cough
Politely, count to five, then doff
One's cap and kiss his diamond ring.
His cooks will diligently bring
In dripping meats to fill his trough,
Which he will gather up and scoff.
Then he will tell his choir to sing,
Waving about his greasy hands
To give his singers their commands.
And once he's deigned to listen to
A fragment of the message you
Have waited hours on end to say,
He orders you to go away.

I'm merely trying to pass on
How bad the councillors all feel
About your losing the Great Seal.
I've told you there was only one
Of us content to see you gone.
We wondered if we could repeal
The law or open an appeal.
We felt the need to act and none
So much as me, I can assure you.
You're busy and I will not bore you
With all the details. I'll just say,
In my opinion, it might pay
To think about what I have said.
Believe me, you are not misled.

WRIOTHESLEY
You would be making a mistake
To guess I cannot see your aim.
I will not play this harmful game.
Did you imagine I would take
Advice from you, you crafty snake?
I marked it when your eyes became
Bright red as though they were aflame.
What raving lunacy could make
You figure that I'm fool enough
To think you bawled into your cuff
When I was ousted by your brother?
You're as self-serving as each other.
Oh yes, Lord Sudeley, you've been seen
Around the all-too-trusting Queen.

You will not keep me here all day.
You've lost. Now make a quick retreat.
Unless I shortly take my seat,
The heretics will hold all sway.
Try as you might, you won't delay
Me any further in this street.
You've failed. Now quickly, on your feet.
Do you not listen? Go away!
You are a smaller man than I,
So hear me when I say goodbye.
Goodbye, Lord Sudeley, fare you well.
Back to your web where spiders dwell.
This is a critical debate
And you've already made me late.

13: *In the King's private rooms at Hampton Court Palace.*

THOMAS SEYMOUR, BARON OF SUDELEY
Are you alone, Your Majesty?
Why are you not attended to?
Have I permission to come through?
You're lucky it is only me.
Any strange fellow would be free
To make his way straight up to you.
Wherever is your retinue?
I simply can't believe that we
Aren't furnished with a single guard
When all the doors are left unbarred.
My residence is always full
And I am just an Admiral.
It is the most outrageous thing.
A man might steal away the King.

KING EDWARD VI
I wonder if you can descry
That Great Dane sleeping over there?
Well, he considers this his lair.
Were someone mad enough to try
To pass dear, friendly Cronus by,
The latter's taste for underwear
Might bring the fellow to despair.
Indeed, I have seen grown men cry
Who've entered in without first knocking.
His antics really are quite shocking.
You're lucky that he is asleep.
I would so hate to see you weep.
He's actually friendly-*ish.*
Play with him, uncle, if you wish.

THOMAS SEYMOUR, BARON OF SUDELEY
He *is* quite friendly? Is that so?
Perhaps, Your Majesty, I'll play
With your Great Dane another day.
I did once have a dog, although
I found it difficult to know
Precisely what I had to say
To get the rascal to obey.
That was, of course, a while ago.
But I'd be just as hopeless now.
It's pitiful, in spite of how
Authoritative my appeal,
I cannot bring a dog to heel.
Nor am I conqueror of nations.
I must respect my limitations.

KING EDWARD VI
Speaking of conquering a nation,
Each night I have been listening
To the new ballads people sing
Outside my window in frustration
Over the lack of information.
Nobody tells me anything.
I might be young but I'm the King.
Must I receive my education
From scoundrels in the street below?
It can't go on. I have to know,
How fares my uncle Somerset?
Have we defeated Scotland yet?
Which lords have fallen? Who lives on?
Do we, at last, have union?

THOMAS SEYMOUR, BARON OF SUDELEY
You look as though you're fit to burst.
I only wish that I could aid
You in some way, but I'm afraid
I'm not especially well-versed
Myself. Alas, I also thirst
For knowledge. I heard tell we made
Light work of putting down some raid
Or other. Somerset dispersed
The rebel forces far and wide.
But who, and quite how many, died,
And whether this amounted to
The battle proper, I'm with you,
Your Majesty, cut off, shut out,
And kept awake at night with doubt.

When I next see him, I'll be sure
To tell it to my brother's face
That it's an absolute disgrace,
Particularly given you're
So agile-minded and mature,
The way you're treated in this place.
I've often wondered why His Grace
Has not invested you with more
Authority in state affairs.
I sometimes question if he cares
At all about Your Majesty.
It's shameful for a king to be
Without the news unless he hears
It sung by half-drunk balladeers.

KING EDWARD VI

You do not know the half of it.
These balladeers have got no class.
Their teeth are desperately sparse.
Their fancy tunics do not fit.
They all wear stockings which are split.
I stood and watched one *scratch his arse*.
Their manners simply will not pass.
You know, I even heard they spit…
I fear that I'll pick up their ways
If there are any more delays
In Somerset's communications.
A king can't hope to rule two nations
If he begins to spend his time
Warbling injunctions in crude rhyme.

Now, uncle, could you spare a groat?
You'll get it back by late this year—
I'm being perfectly sincere.
I meant to scribble you a note.
I'm struggling to keep afloat.
Indeed, I seriously fear
I *will* become a balladeer.
Of course, I positively dote
Upon my uncle Somerset.
However, to my deep regret,
He's rather stingy when it comes
To dishing out the larger sums.
You see, he manages my stash,
And so I'm forced to beg for cash.

THOMAS SEYMOUR, BARON OF SUDELEY

You shouldn't have to supplicate
His Grace for money like a poor,
Obeisant beggar at his door.
My brother keeps you far too straight.
I've never known a head of state
Who's had to beg for groats before.
I've seen him purposely ignore
You, talking idly while you wait
As though you were not there at all,
To make you feel low-down and small.
He thrills to watch his servants stare
Like oxen at you standing there,
Not knowing what you ought to do.
He should be made to come to *you*.

I am completely on your side.
As much as I'm reluctant to
Bring up this trying time anew,
The day your loving father died,
I foolishly imagined I'd
Be charged with looking after you.
But I suppose I always knew
That when the Lord Protector eyed
The opportunity to trap
Another feather for his cap,
He wouldn't let it pass him by.
I do not know the reasons why
My brother is the way he is.
He wishes the whole world were his.

Believe me, nephew I do know
The self-reproaching thoughts which grind
Like rusted cogs within one's mind
When one goes through this puerile show,
Though pride rebukes my saying so.
I still naively hope to find
Some warmth he bears toward mankind,
Albeit buried deep below
The fissures of that martial brain.
Fraternal love attempts in vain
To pitch the virtues of his youth
Into a timeless sphere of truth.
But when he leaves us standing there,
Love can't disguise he doesn't care.

When you want money, come to me.
If you consider it is meet
To boost the lowly in the street,
Just say the word and you will see
That I'll disburse it liberally.
Or should your servants want a treat,
Don't worry, for I am discreet.
Whatever the amount, feel free
To send a brief, informal letter.
On second thoughts, it might be better
If you solicited me here.
Epistles always disappear,
By which I mean they're intercepted,
The King of England's not excepted.

I'm confident we'll find a way.
Let me make certain we're alone…
I always keep some sovereigns sewn
Into my tunic. I will pay
You something, if I can, today.
Remember, this is not a loan.
These sovereigns will be yours to own.
But do not keep them on display.
It would be prudent not to speak
To anyone, apart from Cheke,
About these gifts, you understand?
Come closer and hold out your hand.
How does it feel to see your face
Cast in pure gold instead of base?

These are the very first I've seen
To have been struck in your own mould.
When I acquired them, I was told
I had to keep them all pristine
And so retain that gorgeous sheen.
I think they've made you look quite bold
And actually rather old.
I'd put you at around eighteen.
Or is that too old, would you say?
You do seem older, anyway.
Imagine being fully-grown
And ruling England on your own.
You are already so mature.
You could be doing so much more.

KING EDWARD VI
I *could* be doing so much more.
I would build hospitals and fill
Them with the needy and the ill.
I would have access to a store
Of wealth to raise up London's poor.
I would be able to fulfil
My charge to carry out God's will.
Ah! Being young is such a bore!
It will be good to have the power
To serve my people, *come the hour*.
It is a pity, as you say,
To still be waiting, in a way.
The Duke is predisposed to thrift.
I thank you, uncle, for your gift.

THOMAS SEYMOUR, BARON OF SUDELEY
I think you ought to be prepared
For taking on this future role.
And so does council, on the whole.
My friends have privately declared
That the Duke's power should be shared,
So you can start to take control.
Of course, the council can't cajole
The Duke and, even if we dared
Inform His Grace of our opinion,
He'd never weaken his dominion
Over the offices of state.
It suits my brother to dictate.
He'd rather keep us in submission.
He thinks of *you* as competition.

KING EDWARD VI
Dear uncle, you cannot maintain
That rather silly allegation.
It's totally without foundation.
It is improper to arraign
Your brother when he's on campaign.
You show a strange disinclination
To caution in your conversation.
I'd like to thank you once again.
You have displayed your love for me
With ample generosity.
I think we've both exhausted our
Divergent views on gaining power.
Alas, I am not fully grown,
And now I'd like to be alone.

14: *A letter from Somerset, dictated on the banks of the River Esk, to Paget in London.*

SOMERSET
This note is very overdue.
There is no reason to despair.
I simply had no men to spare,
And it was such a challenge to
Conduct my runners safely through.
But I can now relieve your care.
I have fantastic news to share.
We won, and by some margin, too.
Our terms were, just this morning, sent
Out to the Scottish government.
Negotiations won't be heated,
They are so totally defeated.
In this brief note, I will narrate
Exactly how they met their fate.

But first, I must report Lord Grey
Received a wound straight through his throat,
Quite wide enough to fit a groat.
He and his men were held at bay
By Scottish lancers in the fray.
We thought his chances were remote,
But he was moved onto a boat
And happily saw out the day.
I have got word he's still alive,
And now I'm sure he will survive.
Lord Grey is made of strong, old stuff.
He's a real soldier, rough and tough.
There was no other English lord
So much as grazed by lance or sword.

Lord Arran led the opposition.
No-one can say the man's not brave.
But, like so many, he's a slave
To tired and obsolete tradition.
As such, he is a poor tactician.
He narrowly escaped the grave.
Two nights ago, he boldly gave
My messenger a proposition:
He said he'd fight me, one on one,
And stake success or failure on
A gritty show of martial skill,
By which means we might learn God's will.
I was admittedly amused.
But, naturally, I refused.

As morning broke across the glen,
I found a quiet place and tried
To watch the vapours swirl and glide.
The mist had barely risen when
Lord Arran asked for twenty men
To represent the English side.
I thought this through, still bleary-eyed,
Before refusing once again.
I actually knew that twenty
Of our best champions was plenty
To have ensured a fair result.
However, striving to insult
Your gallant counterpart's ideals
Is only right and just, one feels.

On far-off summits, red deer stirred.
While I have life, I won't forget
Their grand, majestic silhouette.
With prayers and bird-song came the word
Of chivalrous request the third.
It seems I made Lord Arran fret.
Our knight in armour was upset
The contest hadn't been conferred
With the decorum which he saw
As the prerequisite of war.
Lord Arran hoped I would agree
That fifteen-hundred cavalry
Would be sufficient to decide
Upon a final, winning side.

My runner was now out of puff.
He soon began to wheeze and blow,
As if he wished to let me know
That he for one had had enough
Of this preliminary stuff.
His artless features seemed to show
A resolution not to go
If I decided to rebuff
Lord Arran's latest overture.
He somehow managed to say more
In studied silence than in speech,
The way unquestioned fathers teach.
I would have otherwise declined.
But, as fate ordered, I was kind.

The day was now an hour past dawn.
Lord Grey, already on his steed,
Asked my permission to proceed.
I could see then this man was born
To rally to the martial horn.
With Grey positioned at the lead,
The cavalry removed at speed,
Embodying a nation's scorn
With every raging horse's hoof
Stampeding down on Hades' roof.
Their lips curled back; their nostrils flared;
Their eyes were maddened, yet not scared;
Their pounding muscles glistened wet,
Enamelled by hot pools of sweat.

All of a sudden, I was struck
By a most disconcerting fact:
I had committed a rash act.
I had afforded this young buck
An even field to try his luck.
Before our cavalries attacked,
I don't mind saying I was wracked
With fear that we'd become unstuck.
Perhaps I had misjudged Lord Arran.
I questioned, *were* his tactics barren?
I wondered why the thought had never
Occurred to me that he'd been clever
In taking an old-fashioned stance.
Had he not gained a fighting chance?

Perched high atop a grassy knoll,
I kept my eyes intently peeled
For movement on the battle-field.
I hate to play a passive role.
The waiting always takes its toll.
I looked up skyward and appealed
To God to keep my fears concealed.
I *have* to feel I'm in control.
At last, my horsemen reappeared.
Lord Grey's steed turned and proudly reared.
As he was so far out in front,
He personally bore the brunt
Of Arran's cavalry attack.
Although, he gave it all right back.

He pluckily kept up his end
And, after less than half an hour,
Grey had the rascals in his power.
They were unable to defend;
Too spent to aid their nearest friend.
The Scottish cavalry was now a
Bewildered rabble, made to cower.
The wiser soldiers fled to tend
To all their bloody lacerations,
Thereby abandoning their stations-
There was no signal for retreat.
Lord Arran doomed them in defeat
To satisfy a principle,
Thus sanctioning a Scottish cull.

We hacked away as if for fun.
I heard harsh equine screams resound
As Scottish stallions were downed.
I watched the horseless make to run,
While those who were still mounted spun
Their tired and flagging nags around
And dug their heels in for safe ground.
Of course, in theory, we had won
Not just the battle but the war.
However, then my look-outs saw
Great plumes of silver, cloud-like dust
Ascending from the Earth's dried crust.
With an almighty, booming shout,
Lord Warwick cursed them and set out.

The plumes grew high and deep and wide.
The dusty air became opaque.
The ground began to groan and quake.
As my impression clarified,
I learned my counterpart had lied.
Agreements are as quick to break
As they quite often are to make.
Principles can be brushed aside
When kingdoms and eternal fame
Are dangled there for you to claim.
In all its awesome cosmic span,
Has the world made an honest man?
Lord Arran's infantry advanced,
And it was then Lord Grey was lanced.

I'd kept my warships just off-shore.
Lord Warwick hadn't reached the foe,
Therefore I let them stage their show.
Each cannonball smashed through a score
Of Arran's soldiers, if not more.
Foraging widows wouldn't know
Their husbands' flesh from ripped-up dough.
Those spitting iron monsters tore
The devil out of Arran's ranks.
Lord Warwick kindly waved his thanks
And set about the toilsome work
Of fighting with a cheery smirk.
If the war hadn't yet been won,
The battle had, at least, begun.

The hour had sprung to one o'clock.
Still keeping my eyes keenly skinned,
Despite the swirling, dusty wind,
I saw the Scottish run amok
While we stayed solid as a rock.
As Arran's forces slowly thinned,
My infantry was disciplined,
Maintaining an offensive block.
With well-rehearsed commands and signs,
Instructions passed throughout my lines,
And commentaries of attack
Were accurately signalled back.
It was a self-contained machine.
I did not need to intervene.

When the soft calm of evening fell,
The battle, with the day, had cooled.
A honeyed summer lustre pooled
To wish the sky a fond farewell,
And a pink sun began to swell.
The nation which would not be ruled
Had been emphatically schooled.
Lord Warwick sent them all to hell.
Lord Arran, mark you, still lives on.
We searched for him, but he was gone.
He might forget his idiotic
Behaviour under the narcotic
Of every-day, routine affairs.
But what a burden that man bears.

I'm walking now through all the dead.
Some still appear to be awake,
As though death took them by mistake.
Those killed beside the Esk have bled
Into the flow and stained it red.
It favours an exotic snake,
The sort with venoms which would take
Ten seconds flat to reach your head
And dull your speech and blind your sight,
If you should suffer just one bite.
How many thousands lay abroad?
How many slashed by English sword?
Lacking their teeth? their ears? their snout?
With all their clotted brains smashed out?

I want my victory procession
Arranged before my ships set sail-
And on a suitably grand scale.
Don't let the planners make concession
To understatement and discretion.
The taverns must be full of ale.
Let glee and merriment prevail.
I'd also like a special session
Of council to be organised.
I will pretend to be surprised
As all the magnates in the land
Receive me with a rousing hand.
Get going, Paget! Cast your spell.
I trust that I shall find you well.

15: *In Somerset's private rooms at Hampton Court Palace.*

SOMERSET
To be in London at long last!
This is like paradise to me.
It's all a city ought to be.
When I have leisure, I can cast
My mind around within its past,
See everything there is to see,
Let all my thoughts and dreams run free.
London's a city unsurpassed.
How are you, Paget? In good health?
I'm sorry to arrive by stealth.
I thought I'd do the in-bound trip
Aboard a fast and modern ship.
Sailing is pleasanter than riding
On those days when the sun's in hiding.

You're either mightily surprised
Or suffering from some disease.
Relax, my friend, I only tease.
The schedule which I had devised
Was advantageously revised
To catch a favourable breeze
Blasted our way by Ulysses.
I know I should have advertised
My coming better than I did.
But I escaped the giant squid
And all the monsters of the sea.
No harm or mischief came to me,
Except, that is, for my sore throat.
I take it you received my note.

PAGET

I read it through five times or more.
The first time that I quickly scanned
It over, I could hardly stand.
I had to find a bench before
I fell in raptures to the floor.
To have the missive in my hand
That proved we'd hushed that godless land…
Your Grace, it touched me to the core.
I will speed up the preparations
For England's national celebrations.
We'll go about it with attack
Now that I see Your Grace is back.
It is so good to speak with you.
Were your fantastic words all true?

SOMERSET

When my epistle was dictated,
I truly struggled not to tread
On any of the Scottish dead.
The final figure's still awaited,
But fifteen thousand has been stated.
They would have formed a ten-mile thread
If they had fallen foot to head.
I'd say it isn't much inflated.
We have two thousand kept in chains,
Though we're expecting meagre gains.
A few are worth a pound apiece,
A sovereign, maybe, to release.
The farmers' wives will not be willing,
I shouldn't think, to pay a shilling.

We have no gentlemen for sale!
He is a brigand who denies
His bloodied men their well-earned prize.
Although, the contents of our jail
Just goes to show we didn't fail
In our essential enterprise.
Unless they all are in disguise,
They either perished or turned tail,
While I did not expend one lord.
The men will have a fair reward,
Regardless of our ransom pay.
They'll get their dues. I'll find a way.
It will take more than England's dearth
To make me lose my sense of mirth.

PAGET
I'll see the matter is pursued.
No monetary cares should stay
Our soldiers from receiving pay.
I do not want Your Grace's mood
To be at all, as yet, subdued
By what I am about to say.
There are some… *items* to convey.
Domestic woes must not intrude
Upon the gladness of the hour,
Nor turn this national triumph sour.
It is important to be clear:
This has become a golden year,
Not just for us but for the state.
Though there are… *issues* which can't wait.

SOMERSET

What did my wretched brother do?
The very first time I leave town
And we fall victim to that clown.
I faithfully entrusted you
To keep his antics in full view.
Now do not say you've let me down.
Did the great fool attempt the crown
Or settle for a lesser coup?
I tell you, were it up to me,
I'd keep him under lock and key
Whenever I am called away.
How quickly joy becomes dismay
And toleration turns to hate.
What has he done that cannot wait?

PAGET

During the month you were at war,
I am informed the Baron spent
A lot of time near Parliament,
Where one of my best agents saw
Him with the former chancellor.
Your brother wanted to cement
My Lord Wriothesley's discontent,
And made an oath to help him claw
His way back up the greasy pole,
Swearing, indeed, upon his soul.
The meeting didn't last for long
Before they moved into the throng
Of people pouring down the street.
Wriothesley went to take his seat.

Unfortunately, there is more.
The royal tutor, Sir John Cheke,
Thought that he heard your brother speak
As he passed by King Edward's door.
Determined to find out for sure,
He turned the handle with a squeak
And steeled himself to take a peek.
He saw your brother pace the floor,
And there were some gold coins laid out-
A bribe, Your Grace, without a doubt,
Perhaps to tilt the status quo.
But, as things stand, I do not know
Whether this bribe pertains to you
Because Sir John at once withdrew.

SOMERSET
A godly priest would not disperse
Gold coins and ask for nothing back,
Far less a man whose soul is black.
Although, I was expecting worse
Than pledges and an emptied purse.
I am amazed he didn't pack
His Majesty into a sack.
I'll ask the King to reimburse
My brother via Sir John Cheke
So that my brother cannot speak
In private with the King again.
I personally will explain
The matter to His Majesty.
He's really rather fond of me.

If that is all, I will retire.
I'm starting with a dreadful cold
And I am feeling very old.
It is the sum of my desire
To sit beside a roaring fire
And let a jug of wine take hold.
Although my brother has been bold,
The situation isn't dire.
Those dark days after Henry died,
I sat with Edward while he cried.
It is the King's one wish to be
A great commander, just like me.
My exploits fill him with such joy.
I am a hero to the boy.

PAGET
It is still difficult to bring
Myself to think on that event.
You showed a kind and true intent
In sheltering the anguished King
Beneath your soft and gentle wing.
Edward believes you're heaven-sent.
You stopped his woebegone descent.
However, there is one more thing
Which may, or then again may not,
Put stress upon the loaded pot.
The evidence is unconfirmed.
It seems your brother might have wormed
His way into the Queen's affections
With sentimental recollections.

SOMERSET

A violent ardour once rampaged
Throughout their beings like a storm.
But they decided to reform,
And keep their lusty urges caged
Until the cause and object aged.
I'd never witnessed such a swarm
Of passions, lacking any form.
In bloom of youth, they were engaged.
When they were young and immature,
They both seemed too far gone to cure.
They made existence disappear
Through one soft whisper in the ear.
But just as soon as love unfurled,
They both woke up and joined the world.

Is love a cyclical condition
Which can so absolutely burn,
Then unexpectedly return
After a long and calm remission
Without its feeble hosts' volition
To make the passions once more churn?
The realist in me can discern
The shady outline of sedition.
The Queen, of course, is genuine.
She has, perhaps, been taken in
By sweet appeals to love and youth.
In order to sift out the truth
From merely idle speculation,
We must have solid information.

Have they been sleeping with each other?
Has she been cradling his head
As they rest side by side in bed?
Suppose the Queen becomes a mother.
Would she have got it by my brother,
Or by the lifeless King instead?
King Henry is not long since dead.
It would make better sense to smother
The tragic bundle as it naps
Than bounce a time-fuse on our laps.
If this intelligence is true,
We have a lot of work to do.
This towers over everything.
No wonder he has bribed the King.

The chance of crisis is acute,
But we're equipped to meet the need.
I have no doubt that we'll succeed,
Provided we detach the root
Before it lifts the first green shoot.
Together, Paget, we'll proceed
With strength of purpose and with speed.
My brother's schemes will not bear fruit.
He's picked an inauspicious hour
To try the ripeness of my power.
Tomorrow we will cause the news
Of Scotland's conquest to diffuse.
The temper of the populace
Will give his plans a deathly kiss.

Tonight, however, we will rest.
There'll always be some rogue or faction
Demanding swift, decisive action.
We'll never be without a test.
But, in all truth, we have been blessed,
And this is merely a distraction.
We cannot feel dissatisfaction
When Scotland has just been suppressed.
Your phrase has settled in my ear
That this is now a golden year.
We saw our many trials through.
We did what we set out to do.
Like giants, we bestrode the Earth.
Now let's, for once, give in to mirth.

PART TWO

The play continues in summer, 1548.

1: *At the Palace of Westminster.*

PAGET
Unless our absent colleagues sprout
Up from a crevice in the floor,
It seems, my friends, we're only four.
Our falling numbers make me doubt
Whether the plague is near about.
Attendance is extremely poor,
But we can't tarry any more.
At least we will not have to shout
Above the discord of the crowd
Before our speeches are allowed.
It is so quiet in this hall,
Even a mouse within the wall
And a soft-cooing roof-top bird
Can quite distinctly both be heard.

I generally bite my lip
Over these signs of apathy,
Though it's becoming clear to me
That I must take a firmer grip,
As one might say, upon the whip.
I'm sure you *regulars* agree
That councillors should not be free,
As they now think themselves, to skip
These weekly gatherings at will.
Provided they've not fallen ill,
They have a duty to attend.
I know we're coming to the end
Of what has been a vexing year.
Nevertheless, they should be here.

The trouble is they've lost their fire.
If council *has* become a weak,
Inconsequential little clique,
Shouldn't that sorry fact inspire
Us councillors to lift it higher?
If a great ship began to creak
In a bad storm and sprang a leak,
Wouldn't the sailors find some wire
And cloth to stuff into the hole
Sooner than let their vessel roll
Beneath the fury of the waves,
While they swam out for separate caves?
In times of wild and violent weather,
The council has to pull together.

At first their absence marks a stand.
They feel they have a point to prove.
They want to show they disapprove
Of the Duke's absolute command.
But they don't seem to understand
That, once you find an easy groove,
You settle in and cannot move.
A protest which was only planned
To last a week or two goes on
Until a month has been and gone.
Forgetting council, they decide
To travel to the countryside
And, as there's nothing that they lack,
They see no reason to come back.

If he who says he wants a share
In helping draft new legislation
Surrenders to the real temptation
Of leaving us an empty chair,
Then all his oaths are just hot air.
Of course we're bound to feel frustration
About our present situation,
But it's important not to wear
Our troubles with a heavy heart.
We councillors must not depart
Because that only makes things worse.
It's like a self-inflicted curse.
Protesting over the Duke's powers,
We strengthen his and weaken ours.

Enter Warwick

WARWICK
An empty hall! It *is* today,
The meeting, Paget? Where the hell
Is everyone? Not all unwell,
Surely? Perhaps they ran away
When they saw me approach. What say
You my dear friend, Lord Arundel?
My word, those steaming pastries smell
Good. All the more for us then, eh?
A cup of wine is called for I
Believe, don't you? My mouth's bone-dry.
With only five of us, there's no
Point staying, is there? Shall we go
After we've eaten, Paget? I'm
Sure no-one wants to waste their time.

PAGET

I cannot force you to remain.
If you would rather go, then go.
However, I would like to know
What council can expect to gain
By putting business off again.
I don't think cancelling the show
Will make attendance figures grow.
I've been attempting to explain
We need to form a common front
If we are going to confront
The challenges that lie ahead.
A harmful lassitude has spread
Among us like an epidemic.
Indeed, I fear it's now systemic.

ARUNDEL

The reason some are apathetic
Is when, on each blue moon, His Grace,
Our Lord and Master, shows his face,
He's totally unsympathetic.
He treats us like we are pathetic.
He talks to us in that deep bass
Which seems to echo round the place.
His speech is almost homiletic.
We are no longer full-grown men.
We are all little boys again,
With tunics straightened and hair greased,
Standing before the village priest,
Not knowing where we ought to look
As he quotes Scripture from the Book.

My views are always overborne.
I suppose that is my complaint.
Although my notions can be quaint,
That's no excuse to sigh and yawn
And meanly look on me with scorn.
The Duke will never be a saint,
But can't he find some self-restraint?
I'm not some labourer, base-born.
Why can't His Grace be more polite?
To hum a tune is just not right
When one's endeavouring to speak.
One hardly can believe his cheek.
The fellow couldn't be more rude
Or selfish if he hissed and booed.

If council is a ship at sea,
It has already run aground
And all the crew are sadly drowned.
The time the Duke last spoke to me,
The rascal used the royal *we*.
The way he throws his weight around,
You'd think he really had been crowned.
How self-absorbed the man must be
To speak as though he were the King.
I've noticed he has swapped his ring
For one which boasts a larger stone.
Oh yes, this fellow craves the throne.
Have you rode out to see the hall
He's building? It is hardly small.

I thought that council had rejected
His plans to knock that hamlet down
To clear a plot of land in town.
How many families were ejected
For this new hall to be erected?
He has the power of the crown.
When we can only tut and frown,
No wonder some are disaffected.
The people say he loves the poor.
The people wouldn't be so sure
If they could step outside their bubble
And see those homes reduced to rubble,
The tenants not provided for,
Deprived of recourse to the law.

—His wife once tried to make me *bow*!
I saw I had to make a stand.
I said I'd sooner work the land,
Rise with the sun, take up the plough,
Work till sweat beads upon my brow,
Than yield to such a proud demand.
I should have shown the wench my hand-
Intolerable little cow.
That would have put her in her place,
A good, firm slap across the face.
I pay obeisance to the Queen,
Not to a painted figurine
Who's fashioned from a hollow clay
And thinks she holds some kind of sway.

She doesn't speak so much as purr.
She always has that awful, smug
Expression on her ugly mug.
And then she wears that tawdry fur
Which stinks of lavender and myrrh—
Why must she string along that thug
Who trails her like a swollen slug,
Looking admiringly at her,
Fooling himself that each dropped glove
Suggests a deep, unspoken love?
She'll sometimes catch his eye and blink-
Or was it a flirtatious wink?
And thus the knave's left wanting more.
The Duchess is a vain, old whore.

THOMAS SMITH
While my dear colleague clears his throat,
There's something I would like to say.
Returning briefly, if I may,
To Paget's image of a boat,
I am convinced we're still afloat.
If the old soldier had his way,
There would be *no-one* here today.
So let's be thankful and devote
The time remaining to debate.
Arranging yet another date
On which to hold this council meeting,
As Paget said, is self-defeating.
We cannot hope to fix attendance
Until we show some independence.

PAGET
Although we're numbered only five,
I just as ardently object
To the idea we are wrecked.
So long as we all firmly strive
To keep our sundry roles alive,
I'm strongly given to suspect
That we will win the Duke's respect
And, in the future, once more thrive.
With Smith's injunction to commence
Urbanely ushering us hence,
We'll save the finer points of law
Until we have thrashed out the war
Which, since it dawned a year ago,
Has been the cause of all our woe.

2: *In Somerset's private rooms at Whitehall Palace, where King Edward is keeping court.*

SOMERSET
I am not feeling at my best.
Please do not make too loud a sound,
Or you will cause my head to pound.
Last night I was Lord Warwick's guest.
He put my liver to the test.
It is a wonder how I found
My bed. The room was spinning round
So fast, I couldn't get undressed.
Once I had tossed aside my hat,
I hit the sheets and that was that.
We only drank the proper stuff
But, even so, it's left me rough.
If I recall, he made a fleeting
Mention of some or other meeting…

PAGET
You missed a meeting yesterday.
The gathering was very small.
Five councillors were there in all.
Preferring the soft life of play,
Most of the rest have gone away.
Yet those remaining caused a squall
To shake the rafters in that hall.
I listened to them with dismay.
It seemed that everyone who spoke
Complained of how the country's broke.
The Scottish rebels can't be beat.
When will the Duke accept defeat?
The Lord Protector doesn't care.
Why is it that you were not there?

SOMERSET
Paget, I'd nothing to report.
It would be pointless to rehearse
How things have gone from bad from worse
Since France decided to support
Those heathens at the Scottish court.
We're all aware of the adverse
Effect war's having on our purse.
The council knows there's not a fort
That isn't under close attack,
Causing us to be driven back.
They understand the men are fed
On stewed-up oats and rock-hard bread
And, for their troubles, take no pay.
I don't know what you'd have me say.

PAGET
I'd have you say it can't go on.
Much to the councillors' frustration,
You think of war as recreation.
Picture the soldiers who have gone
To our main base at Haddington.
Imagine their sheer desperation.
They're in a state of near starvation.
Give lives and faces to each one.
Picture them there now in the glen.
They're not just numbers, they are men.
Enable every void to find
A human profile in your mind,
Dreaming of meat, a drop of beer.
We've been at war for one whole year.

SOMERSET

Indeed it has been one whole year.
The Earth, as some believe, has spun
Another circuit round the sun.
However, I can't shed a tear
For soldiers who have got no beer.
Were they expecting to have fun?
War's war when all is said and done.
It's hunger, death and constant fear.
It isn't my fault life's not fair.
The truth is most of them don't care,
Don't even stop to think about
Their drink and foodstuffs running out.
Nor are they terribly concerned
To have the money they have earned.

PAGET

Then tell me, when your soldiers wake
To face another day of dread,
With itching eyes, puffed-up and red,
With necks and backs which sorely ache,
Hands which perpetually shake,
Limbs weighing heavier than lead,
What motive gets them out of bed?
What cause, what stimulus can make
A man endure the hell of war?
If most of them aren't fighting for
The basic needs of food and drink,
And if they do not stop to think
About the wages they are due,
Why do they care to see it through?

SOMERSET

They persevere despite the drain
Upon the body and the mind
Occasioned by the daily grind
That goes with being on campaign,
As they develop strength through pain-
An optimism of a kind.
The chaos strangely helps you find
A unity with God again
As, burning through the mists of fear,
Religion suddenly glares near.
Undoubtedly, it's always there.
But now it almost seems to flare
Like the sun's heat against your face
And things fall neatly into place.

It isn't easy to explain
But, when you feel yourself inclined
To shirk the duties you're assigned,
Lacking the spur of worldly gain;
When motivation starts to wane,
And your blood-crusted brow is lined
With thoughts of what you've left behind,
Christian worship will sustain
You in its warmth and piercing light.
The knowledge that you're in the right,
That you are working for a cause,
Upholding the Almighty's Laws
In life and death through word and deed
Is all the sustenance you need.

PAGET

I am afraid I don't agree.
The men primarily need pay,
And food delivered straight away.
I think you're making fun of me,
Speaking of Christianity.
Running the risk of death each day
Possibly does make soldiers pray.
I just don't think that God's the key.
If you'll forgive my saying so,
There was a time not long ago
When you spoke only common sense:
Supply routes, tactics, pounds and pence.
The man you used to be would baulk
To hear such wishy-washy talk.

SOMERSET

A statesman cannot comprehend
These things unless he's been and fought.
Why won't you let yourself be taught?
Their loyalty does not depend
On having petty cash to spend.
A soldier's honour can't be bought.
Pennies and pounds are things of nought.
They fight to serve a higher end.
Until the day when they're dismissed,
They will continue to subsist,
Making the most of what's at hand
And scavenging the war-torn land
In whatsoever ways they can.
They will stay constant to a man.

Success is never purchased cheap.
I will admit we're battle-scarred.
But when the way ahead seems barred,
We don't collapse into a heap,
Cry out for beer and start to weep.
We move on forwards, yard by yard,
So-be-it desperately hard.
We meet each challenge and we keep
On pushing with renewed desire.
When soldiers wake, they build a fire;
They find a stream to fill their flasks;
Then they complete their daily tasks.
There is no *where's my food and pay*.
And trust me, Paget, they do pray.

PAGET
Oh, very well. They're all devout.
They sing their prayers into the sky
With their knees bent and hands raised high.
But how do soldiers go about
Filling their flasks when there's a drought
That's made the streams and brooks run dry?
And, if the Scottish are nearby,
Then how can soldiers venture out
Upon this daily expedition,
Given their lack of ammunition?
It isn't to control their fear
That they are crying out for beer.
The reason, Somerset, is, first
And foremost, agonizing thirst.

It hurts me being stern with you.
You're not a mean or heartless man.
I'm sure you're doing all you can
To get provisions running through.
I have no wish to turn the screw.
It's just that since the war began,
We've never had a proper plan.
Your victory did not subdue
The rebels as we thought it would.
On that one day, we spilled the blood
Of over fifteen thousand men.
Yet Scotland raised itself again
And, with tremendous force of will,
Is standing in defiance still.

I've only one more thing to say.
Although it leaves him much aggrieved,
Seeing as little's been achieved,
The man *who's there*, your friend, Lord Grey,
Advises calling it a day.
In the last letter you received,
He asked once more to be relieved.
In his opinion, there's no way
That we can forge a union.
He tells you straight, all hope is gone.
When an old fighter, rough and tough
In your words, says enough's enough
And we should cut our project short,
It ought to give us pause for thought.

SOMERSET
Lord Grey is on his final lap
Around a long and gruelling track.
I'll soon invite him to come back.
He's fought in many a hard scrap
And I have never seen him flap.
Under continual attack,
However, anyone can crack.
It is a feather in his cap
That he is even there at all.
If you are able to recall,
He had a pike rammed through his jaw
At the beginning of the war.
When he's relieved of his command,
I'll be the first to shake his hand.

Here's what we'll do, we'll set a date:
One month from now. I'll put aside
My airs and my appalling pride
And we will have a good debate.
The councillors can put me straight.
I will permit them to deride
Every last measure I've applied.
I'll tell them there's no need to skate
Around the hotter points, all meek
And mild. They'll have the chance to speak
Their minds as though I were not there.
Now, my dear Paget, is that fair?
If you agree my scheme's a winner,
I think that makes it time for dinner.

3: *At Thomas Seymour's residence, Holt Castle, situated on the Welsh-English border.*

THOMAS SEYMOUR, BARON OF SUDELEY
Lord Warwick, shall we take the air?
You must excuse the mess outside.
The castle's being fortified.
These blasted masons everywhere
Have nearly brought me to despair,
But Catherine's not to be denied.
The recent threat of nationwide
Upheavals gave her quite a scare.
Although the danger fizzled out,
My wife was keen to set about
Creating a safe haven for
Our unborn child lest civil war
Should cruelly bring him to his doom
While he's still in his mother's womb.

Though rural anarchy is rife,
I can't conceive an angry throng
Of country folk will come along
And try to bring us all to strife.
It wasn't for a quiet life,
However, that I held my tongue.
There are some shining gems among
The many qualities my wife
Has been hand-picked by God to own.
Her startling prescience alone
Would wholly warrant my submission.
Not merely woman's intuition,
The Queen has almost an innate
Capacity to uncloak fate.

If, God forbid, the Queen is right
That peasants will start making stands,
That discontented working hands
Will set the country hall alight
To make the greedy squire take flight,
And organise their separate bands
In order to produce demands,
This seething isle will host a fight
To break the sleep of history.
Alas! You haven't learned from me!
Will sound a sad, paternal moan.
My castle will need all the stone
The quarries can yield up and more
Should such commotion lie in store.

Of course, it hasn't happened yet.
Although it's still a mystery,
Incomprehensible to me,
Why people think they owe a debt
Of gratitude to Somerset.
Why is it no-one seems to see
The greater part of all that we
Have ample reason to regret,
The currency devaluation,
Excessive levels of taxation,
The soaring price of grain and meat,
The beggars dying in the street,
All this has issued from his war?
He has a lot to answer for.

He's brought this country to its knees.
I fear that I'm at odds with you,
But pardon me, my friend, it's true.
The local squires are ill at ease.
They haven't met with times like these,
So full of worry, hitherto.
I've tried to think what I can do,
Beyond attempting to appease
The trouble-makers in these parts,
Those who have mischief in their hearts.
But I am helpless, I regret.
It all comes down to Somerset.
The problem is he thinks that he's a
Reincarnated Roman Caesar.

WARWICK
We're not at odds, Sir Thomas. You're
An honest man to speak your mind
Thus. Our opinions are aligned.
The country cannot take much more
Of this. It won't be long before
Men such as those around us find
A leader they can get behind.
It's necessary to ensure
The safety of our loved ones. I
Am also fortifying my
Castle. It's madness, isn't it?
The very masons who now split
And lay these stones will likely try
To pulverize them, by and by.

I've stuck by Somerset through thick
And thin. The Lord Protector's my
Old friend. Although, quite frankly, I
Think I'm becoming a bit sick
Of him. It cuts me to the quick
To say this, but I cannot lie.
I am not willing to stand by
And watch as time begins to tick
Towards disaster. As you say,
The Scottish war has run away
From him. I told him that it would.
I counselled him, for all the good
It did, to chuck the whole thing in.
But no. He still thinks he can win.

THOMAS SEYMOUR, BARON OF SUDELEY
Lord Warwick, since you wrote to say
That you'd be visiting me here,
I've been beside myself with fear
Over the purpose of your stay,
So much so, earlier today
Watching your carriage drawing near,
My instinct was to disappear
And make out I'd been called away.
But for my muscles going slack,
I would have ran and not looked back.
I deemed no cause, no explanation
Too silly for consideration.
You know I even weighed the reason
That you suspected me of treason!

I thought perhaps I shouldn't speak
About my brother's folly lest
Your coming was some kind of test.
As I embarked on my critique,
My terror therefore reached its peak.
I felt so hopelessly distressed,
My heart was beating through my chest.
Indeed it's left me rather weak.
Thank heavens, though, I didn't shrink
From saying what I truly think.
It means the entire world to me
To have a man like you agree
With my opinion of the Duke.
And do you offer no rebuke?

WARWICK
Do I not offer you a what?
Rebuke? A telling off? Why no,
Lord Sudeley! Surely you now know
The council's on your side. It's not
A crime, nor is it any blot
Upon your character to show
Your natural concern. We owe
You one for firing the first shot,
In fact. I couldn't say so in
The note I sent, but I have been
Craving the opportunity
To come to Holt. You have to see,
If there is anybody who
Can save this country, it is you.

THOMAS SEYMOUR, BARON OF SUDELEY
This leaves me utterly aghast.
My hints have never before found
The channels of such fertile ground.
Is my ill-favour in the past?
Can it be true that I've at last
Begun to win the council round?
Am I so loved, so well-renowned,
That my dear friends see fit to cast
Me in my country's leading role-
Or would I share the Duke's control?
Neither, of course. It cannot be.
You've made a perfect fool of me.
Did I say something to provoke
This rather cruel and thoughtless joke?

WARWICK
Lord Sudeley, I would never joke
About my country's future in
Such flippant terms. If I have been
Speaking in jest, then may I choke
Upon my words. The country's broke,
And the fact is we must begin
To fix it. It would be a sin
To suffer meekly the Duke's yoke
Of tyranny. I'll say again,
I'm representing some good men
Who favour you and it is our
Belief that you should have more power.
In black and white, we'd like to bring
You greater access to the King.

—Hold on! Don't tell me what you think
Until I've finished. There is more.
In order to confirm where your
Best chances lay, I had a drink
With Somerset. I let him sink
What must have been about a score,
At least, of cups of beer before
I asked him, with a friendly wink,
Whether he really will address
The council next time. He said yes,
For once he really will. So that
Means we can hit him when he's at
His weakest, being shredded for
Prolonging his disastrous war.

When the Duke takes his place, we'll let
The councillors interrogate
Him. We will follow the debate
In silence. We won't pounce as yet.
Your secret friends will make him sweat.
When the reproofs begin to grate
Against his ego, we will wait
A little longer, then we'll set
Upon him like a pair of wild
Cats. You'll ask council to be styled
Officially as Governor
To the King's person. As the claw
Of justice latches on, I'll back
You up and finish the attack.

He will be made to understand
That he is beaten. Clouds of steam
Will issue from him. He will deem
It treachery. But, if we stand
Together just as I have planned,
There is no reason why our scheme
Should not succeed. The Duke's regime,
Like all its kind, is built on sand.
He is a tyrant. He's upset
Too many people. I regret
All this as much as you do, but
There's no alternative. He's shut
Us out, Lord Sudeley. Tell me what
You're thinking. Am I talking rot?

THOMAS SEYMOUR, BARON OF SUDELEY
I'm mainly thinking that I must
Be very careful where I tread.
I have to keep a level head.
You've taken me into your trust
And I'm convinced our cause is just.
However, I am full of dread.
Is there a safer way instead?
It seems to be win all or bust—
I need some time. I need to think.
Let's go inside and have a drink.
With all these masons darting near us,
There is a chance they'll overhear us.
I wish the rascals would be gone.
Proceed, my lord. I'll follow on.

4: *At the Palace of Westminster.*

SOMERSET
Friends, I've attempted to restore
The faith that you once had in me.
You've listened very patiently
Indeed. My thanks for that. Before
I shortly open up the floor
To questions- and please do feel free
To speak your minds- I ask to be
Permitted to say one thing more.
As everybody surely knows,
It's been a year of highs and lows,
Substantially, alas, the latter.
I cannot represent the matter
Of war in Scotland otherwise.
To do so would be telling lies.

However, we are on the verge
Of conquering a new domain.
Our efforts haven't been in vain.
The patient just needs once more purge
And then I know we will emerge
Triumphant from this long campaign.
The rebels' strength is on the wane.
As always, therefore, I must urge
My councillors to stay the course.
Pulling our keen and eager force
Out of the glens of Scotland now
Is something we cannot allow.
Retreat would damage not just me,
But also Henry's legacy.

ARUNDEL

I have a question for Your Grace.
The progress of your war is dire,
But people say God loves a trier.
I'd like to ask about your face.
How do you fix that smile in place?
Do you employ a bit of wire
To keep your cheek-bones lifted higher?
Because, if that should be the case,
I've often thought I'd benefit
From having the same gadget fit.
These past twelve months, I've aged ten years.
Looking around, I think my peers,
If they'll forgive my saying so,
Would also rather like to know.

PAGET

How shall we lighten up the mood?
My belly's rumbling like thunder.
We haven't eaten yet! No wonder.
Where's our display of tempting food?
I find my judgement can be skewed
And I'm more liable to blunder
Without a tableful of plunder.
The pangs of hunger can intrude
Upon a normally calm wit
Like an involuntary fit.
Lord Warwick, would you ring the bell?
Thank heavens! Now, Lord Arundel,
I fear I'm interrupting. Pray,
Tell council what you have to say.

ARUNDEL

My conscience prompts me to repeat
Exactly what I have just said.
Is that smile fixed into your head?
No, Paget! *You* can take a seat.
What kind of man would ring for meat?
We do not want a wasteful spread.
Our soldiers only get stale bread
And chopped-up vegetables to eat.
Was it your aim to calm me down?
Well I intend to go to town
Upon the Duke, our lord and master's,
Up-till-today unsung disasters.
Yes, you may well look to His Grace.
You'll see I've built up quite a case.

To start with, I have been informed
Of a near-ruinous affair.
You likely will be unaware
That Haddington was almost stormed.
A mob of Scottish wastrels swarmed
Into the central passage where
They could have accessed the main square.
Our soldiers fortunately warmed
Them up somewhat with pots of oil
Which they'd been keeping on the boil—
But not before they entered, mark.
The Duke has kept us in the dark
About this sorry episode.
Was this to ease the council's load?

THOMAS SEYMOUR, BARON OF SUDELEY

I think, my lord, it's safe to say
We cannot pin the reason there.
We all have so much time to spare
That most of us have gone away
To give ourselves to idle play.
My brother takes the lion's share
Of business into his own care
And so we find no cause to stay.
As you, my lord, already know,
We feel our load like flakes of snow,
Or like unfinished strands of flax
Coming to rest upon our backs.
Not out of our consideration
Has he kept back this information.

Embarrassment? Incompetence?
Of all the words which I could use,
It's hard to know which one to choose.
Why bother making a defence
When you can simply build a fence
Of secrecy around bad news?
Stepping into my brother's shoes,
This all amounts to common sense.
There's no deceit in operation.
My brother has no obligation
To tell us menials a thing.
The Duke is England's second King
And we must treat his word as law
Where it concerns his blessèd war.

PAGET
Let's call a temporary truce.
Nobody here is made of stone
And that was very near the bone.
There's absolutely no excuse
For falling back upon abuse.
The Duke does not share Edward's throne.
We have one King and one alone.
Why hurt each other? What's the use?
Let us continue this debate
As sober councillors of state.
Lord Arundel has brought to light
That there has been a bitter fight
Inside the walls of our main fort.
This is a valuable report.

The central issue now at hand
Is by what means can we prevent
Another such surprise event.
This wasn't just a local stand.
It clearly must have been well-planned.
How did the rebels circumvent
Our earthworks after all we've spent
On building traps into the land?
How did they pass our killing field,
Where there's no tree or bush to shield
A warily approaching foe?
These are all things we have to know.
I vote we send Lord Grey a letter
To help us grasp the problem better.

THOMAS SEYMOUR, BARON OF SUDELEY
The Duke of Somerset has lied.
I won't allow you to distract
The council from this basic fact.
Lost in the luxury of pride,
The Lord Protector chose to hide
The news that we have been attacked.
An English fort was nearly sacked.
Why do you take my brother's side?
I am amazed you cannot see
We need accountability—
Whatever you have got to say,
Please save if for another day.
We've listened to the fawning pet.
Now let us hear from Somerset.

SOMERSET
Dear brother, you have had your sport.
Be seated. I have not deceived
A soul. The moment I received
The news, I read the full report
Verbatim to the royal court.
Although the King was much aggrieved,
In view of what I have achieved
So far, His Majesty's support
For my endeavours was renewed.
I can forgive your being rude,
Lord Sudeley and Lord Arundel.
I'm certain that you both meant well.
I understand you're cross with me,
But I did tell His Majesty.

THOMAS SEYMOUR, BARON OF SUDELEY

And that makes everything okay?
I'm glad the King has granted you
His token patronage anew.
That doesn't, brother, mean to say
You've acted in a proper way.
A Lord Protector's bounden to
Inform the privy council too,
Or else our function will decay.
We have to know what's going on.
Suppose they'd captured Haddington
And cruelly butchered all our men.
Would you have told the council then?
How does Lord Somerset decide
What news to share and what to hide?

I expect I would likely shrug
My shoulders too in your position.
The truth will not bear exposition.
Let's see if this'll wipe that smug
Expression from your ugly mug:
Wise council, I'm no rhetorician,
But through a wild, uncurbed ambition,
The Duke of Somerset has dug
The land I love into a hole.
As such I ask to have control
Of the King's person from now on.
We can no longer suffer one
Man's bursting ego to inflate
Into each chamber of the state.

Although my nephew is wide-eyed,
Indeed he's not yet twelve years old,
He is intelligent and bold.
My brother is too strict a guide.
I'd let His Majesty decide
Himself what values to uphold.
He doesn't need to be controlled.
Whilst I believe I'm qualified
To undertake this vital role,
I am not able to extol
Whatever virtues I possess.
Perhaps my friends will now express
The constitution of my heart.
Lord Warwick, would you care to start?

WARWICK
We're wasting time. My Lord, what date
Did the aforesaid siege occur?
Why did our archers not deter
Them from advancing? Our main gate
Is made to stand ten tonnes in weight
Before it gives. Perhaps we were
The victim of a saboteur:
A Scottish spy who let them straight
In. Paget said it best. There's no
Point laying blame. We have to know
The precise details of the raid
So that improvements can be made—
And if Lord Sudeley tries to tell
Us different, he can go to hell.

THOMAS SEYMOUR, BARON OF SUDELEY
Lord Sudeley can go where? to hell?
Repeat yourself. You talk in Greek.
I am your dearest friend. Come, speak!
Correct me. Warwick, you're not well.
You're not yourself. Some harmful spell
Has severed speech from thought. Last week
At Holt you welcomed my critique
Of this false tyrant. Arundel,
Lord Arundel, take up my case.
Discourse upon that smirking face
Again. Continue on your theme.
You must be privy to our scheme.
I have support. He told me so.
He told me not five days ago.

ARUNDEL
You certainly do not have mine.
Lord Sudeley at the royal court!
No, you do not have my support
As you well know, you artful swine.
Lord Warwick, pass that jug of wine.
Touching improvements to the fort,
I'd like to add to my report
By saying Haddington's design
Appears to be entirely sound.
The rebels therefore must have found
Some means to introduce a spy.
With council's leave, I will now try
To summarize my thoughts about
How we can root the devil out…

5: *At Holt Castle.*

CATHERINE PARR
The beast has risen from the mire!
I wondered if you were awake.
Did you observe the new dawn break?
I don't suppose I'll ever tire
Of seeing darkness turn to fire.
I thought I'd treat myself and take
The spectacle in by the lake.
Watching the sun climb slowly higher
Is mother-nature's sweetest balm.
It seems to promise that no harm
Will come to those who fuel their days
By soaking up its gentle rays.
It is a most relaxing sight.
I trust, my love, you slept last night?

THOMAS SEYMOUR, BARON OF SUDELEY
My shoulders ache, my neck feels tight
And my eyes tickle when I blink.
I barely slept a single wink.
I also watched the morning light
Balloon itself upon the night.
The thirsty dawn appeared to drink
The bluing darkness like spilt ink.
It's only a relaxing sight
When it has followed peaceful rest.
I contemplated getting dressed
But, conquering my urge to rise,
I once more shut my weary eyes
And counted several flocks of sheep.
I managed fifteen minutes' sleep.

How did Lord Warwick have the gall,
The cheek, the hubris to pretend
To be my closest, dearest friend?
He gave me no support at all.
I've never felt so lost and small.
He said, he *promised* he'd defend
Me up until the bitter end.
I dreamt that I was in that hall,
Unable to escape my shame.
It all proceeded much the same,
Except I used high-pitched screech
With which to make my wretched speech.
I woke with Warwick's *go to hell*,
Which sent me breathless to my cell.

Why does the sleeping mind explore
The things we'd rather just forget?
We aren't content unless we fret.
If the Duke hated me before,
He must now loathe me even more.
It is to my profound regret
That I've been caught in Warwick's net.
Lord Warwick's emblem is the boar,
But he is subtler than that.
He's like a sneaky, unseen rat,
An animal you do not fear
Until those blood-red spots appear.
Still unsuspected by my brother,
He's pitching us against each other.

Perhaps he is the tool of fate.
I'm growing sick of politics,
With all its plotting, schemes and tricks.
How can it be a noble state
Is run by men who feed on hate?
There is a painting which depicts
Us statesmen on the River Styx:
That captures how I feel of late,
As though my vessel has been hurled
Into a murky underworld
And on we row into the dark.
That image is so near the mark,
I've often thought I should retire,
Lest the ship burns in Hades' fire.

But every man's a politician,
Contriving in his own small way
To gain a modicum of sway.
The world is one big competition
In which we jockey for position,
Not caring who we lead astray,
Trampling over who we may.
We're all made villains by ambition,
And who am I to lay the blame?
All people are, in truth, the same:
We're selfish, ruthless, mean and hard.
In tailor's shop and tanner's yard,
In baron's court and strumpet's bed,
Men lie and cheat to get ahead.

Ask me what right have I to vent
The victim's rage at anyone
And I would have to answer none.
For many months now I've been bent
On vainly plotting my ascent.
I positively leaped upon
The grave report from Haddington.
That news, to me, seemed heaven-sent.
How terrible a thing to say!
I'm worse than Warwick in a way.
I have been burdened with the wit
To know that I'm a hypocrite.
I pray you will enlighten me,
Am I the rascal or is he?

CATHERINE PARR
You are the kindest man I know.
You were exploited and misled.
However, what's been said's been said.
You have received a bitter blow
And now you have to let it go.
If sad thoughts creep into your head,
Think of our unborn child instead.
You're a good person and you owe
It to yourself to filter out
These worthless afterthoughts of doubt.
If I may give you some tough love,
I'd say you have to rise above
The scheming of that drunken clown.
You mustn't let him get you down.

THOMAS SEYMOUR, BARON OF SUDELEY

As always, Catherine, you are right.
There is no point in feeling sad.
I'm sure that, after I have had
A good eight hours of sleep tonight,
I will be equal to my plight.
I'll dream about our little lad.
The thought that I will be a dad
Affords me with as much delight
As anyone has ever known.
Let the Duke covet Edward's throne.
Let Warwick aim at my disgrace.
Whatever my allotted place
In the Almighty's master-plan,
I am a very lucky man.

6: *In the state rooms of the first newly-built wing of Somerset House.*

SOMERSET

I'll tell you now that you will lose
If you intend to challenge me.
On that you have my guarantee.
It has long since become old news
That we possess divergent views
Regarding the economy.
You say the country's all at sea.
You even hint that I abuse
The coinage to draw out my war.
You are the wasted mouthpiece for
Those who think every pound I spend
Advancing that so-called dead-end
Is money thrown into a pit.
I argue quite the opposite—

Please, for one moment, hold your tongue.
Though food costs reached historic highs,
They are no longer on the rise.
When the fine weather came along,
Our good old farmers bounced back strong.
God gave us sunny, cloudless skies,
And we rebuilt our grain supplies.
Ask any farmer if I'm wrong.
The barns of England are all full-
That's saying nothing about wool,
Which we're producing in great sacks.
The people don't mind paying tax
So long as they are doing well.
A rich man never did rebel.

THOMAS SMITH
I'm not so proud that I insist
On my opinions being right.
I do not wish to start a fight.
I am here simply to assist
Your Grace as your economist.
It is my job to shed some light
On fiscal measures which you might
Have over-hastily dismissed,
As busy as you no doubt are
With sundry other matters far
More salient in kind than these.
If I in any way displease,
I will be happy to defer
To your more expert judgement, sir.

SOMERSET
That was an unforeseen admission.
I'm strongly given to suspect
Those who display too much respect.
They're either guilty of sedition
Or they are bearing a petition.
You ought to know that I expect
Advisors to be more direct.
You need not offer your submission,
Nor waste time sugaring the pill.
You will not earn my trust until
You can say plainly what you think.
I'll pour us both a little drink.
Have you seen Paget recently?
There is a man who's straight with me.

THOMAS SMITH
I've been informed that he has fled
To the West Midlands with his wife
In order to preserve his life.
The rumour is that someone said
They wanted to see Paget dead.
One can't say violence isn't rife.
I'm told a fellow threw a knife
At a priest, aiming for his head,
As he was stood outside St Paul's.
The fellow thought the market stalls
Would give him cover to escape.
They caught him purchasing a cape.
The preacher came to no real harm.
The dagger only grazed his arm.

SOMERSET
If it had hit him on the crown
And spilled his brains, I wouldn't care.
Why do you speak of St Paul's square?
You say that Paget has left town?
I can't believe he'd let me down.
You mentioned the West Midlands. Where
In the West Midlands? Beaudesert,
His seat? Did someone of renown
Issue the threat, or was it just
A rascal in the street? It must
Have been a magnate, or else why
Would he have felt the need to fly
To safety? It's outrageous he
Should scarper and abandon me.

THOMAS SMITH
I do not think we need concern
Ourselves. As soon as Paget sees
White clouds, blue waters and green trees,
I'd bet ten guineas he will yearn,
Like a lost pilgrim, to return.
He suffers from a rare disease:
Paget is only at his ease
When he is able to discern
No colours save for London grey
Outside his window. One more day,
Your Grace, and he'll be back again,
Scuttling head-down through the rain
To meet with you. Now should we be
Reviewing the economy?

SOMERSET
Yes, Smith, we should. Perhaps you're right.
Paget will find no relaxation
From spending time in isolation.
He'll come back shortly. I will write
A friendly note to him tonight
To clarify the situation.
I am still cross he's left his station,
Mark you. A man should stand and fight.
When under threat, you show some heart.
You do not jump into your cart
And speed off to your country house
Like a pathetic, frightened mouse.
However, he will not be gone
For very long, so let's get on.

THOMAS SMITH
Your Grace has touched upon the worth
Of wool and foodstuffs, namely grain.
It's true that farmers in the main
Were briefly this year full of mirth.
God didn't choose to flood the Earth.
We had warm sun instead of rain,
Which gave the soil a chance to drain.
And yet we do still have a dearth.
The countryside is not in health.
Most farmers haven't kept their wealth.
When squire sees farmer kiss the ground,
The rent goes up another pound.
Most working rural folk would scoff
At the idea they're well-off.

We can't, however, blame the squire,
Who's only trying to recoup
His losses to the merchant group.
The goods which country gents desire
Have recently been priced much higher
As home production starts to droop.
So all are caught in one great loop.
There's not a city, town or shire
That isn't now in disrepair,
And neither state nor church can care
For those in poverty and dying,
Although God knows how hard we're trying.
A problem therefore does exist.
The signs of hardship can't be missed.

—You're happy for me to proceed?
Then it's important we should pause
To fix upon the dearth's root cause.
Here preachers often take the lead
In staking out a case for greed,
Calling on us to make tough laws.
This may well win the crowd's applause,
But I'm inclined to think we need
The stimulus of avarice.
The argument boils down to this:
As selfishness is nothing new,
Why did the country not go through
The present dearth last century?
That's where the priest trips up for me.

Would Your Grace say I'm being fair?
So what, or who, then is to blame
If men have always been the same.
We clearly have to look elsewhere
To lay this tricky matter bare.
If you would suffer a bold claim,
Then I will give Your Grace a name.
I'm doing this because I care.
I've been instructed not to prate.
Therefore I'll tell it to you straight.
The man whose policies gave birth
To this unwanted monster, dearth,
Is you, the Duke of Somerset.
Your war has placed us all in debt.

It wounds me deeply to rehearse
This but, as far as I'm concerned,
Scotland has ruined us. It's turned
Into a washout. It's a curse,
A ceaseless drain upon our purse.
We're spending cash we haven't earned.
I am afraid to say you've spurned
All sound advice and, what is worse-
To me at least, is that you've told
The minters to recast our gold
Coins with more copper. People see
The image of His Majesty
And laugh. Our coins are so debased,
The King stares out at us red-faced.

SOMERSET
This is the way that I would put
It: Yes, for every Scot we kill,
There's half a bag of charge to fill.
It's costly. Scotland's a tough nut
To crack. They're stubborn. Yet my gut
Tells me that England surely will
Come through. We'll fight with pike and bill
When all the powder's gone. We'll cut
Them up with swords or else with knives.
Good soldiers can snuff out men's lives
With anything that comes to hand.
You've heard they're living off the land
Without their pay? That saves us quite
A bit. We'll win. I know I'm right.

Smith, I am glad you came today.
You've given me a lot to think
About. Please finish up your drink.
Alas, my mind's begun to stray.
It irks me that he's gone away.
I thought a man like him would wink
At danger. Only cowards shrink
Into the shadows. I won't say
I miss him. No! I will not beg.
Never! I'll take him down a peg
Or two. I'll make him see he's let
Me down. If I received a threat,
I would— Well, anyway, goodbye,
Smith. I am grateful you stopped by.

7: *At Holt Castle.*

GENTLEMAN-IN-WAITING
I have refused, for both our sakes,
To please my lady with a child.
I said she mustn't be beguiled
By young boys playing ducks and drakes
And going boating on blue lakes.
In public, they are sweet and mild.
But when they're home, they all run wild.
I told her they'll become cads, rakes,
Bent villains who don't earn a wage
And rob their parents in old age.
Of course, it made no difference.
A brooding woman can't see sense.
To my dismay, she's still as keen.
Well, such is life. How fares the Queen?

THOMAS SEYMOUR, BARON OF SUDELEY
She's been in labour for twelve hours.
I didn't sleep a wink last night.
I left my quarters at first light
And went to visit her rose-bowers.
Catherine adores those hardy flowers.
Not one has fallen prey to blight.
They have remained washed-linen white.
I wish this harassed love of ours
Could weather nature's huffs and blows
As smoothly as the garden rose.
I love the Queen as much as ever.
It didn't cross my mind, however,
That I'd be subject to her wrath
When we set out upon this path.

She's gentle; then she's full of scorn.
One moment happy; the next sad.
Is it some kind of modish fad
For ladies to wake up at dawn
And eat a bowl of buttered corn,
Or has this baby sent her mad?
I tell you, I'll be very glad
When the young trouble-maker's born.
It isn't just her shifting moods
Or her obsession with queer foods
That has exasperated me.
I sometimes think this pregnancy
Has come to dominate my life
And almost robbed me of my wife.

Add to the mix my brother's guile,
Wishing us all the very best
While spitting oaths into his breast,
And it's all felt like one big trial.
However, it has been worthwhile.
We kept our faith and God has blessed
Us with a chick to grace our nest.
Of course, he'll have his mother's smile.
I hope he'll also have her eyes,
Still pretty, even when she cries.
It would be terribly unfair
If he receives my ginger hair.
In fact the less he takes from me,
The better off the boy will be!

That equally applies to school.
Despite my having been athletic,
At home with numbers, and poetic,
My strengths and weaknesses were dual.
I launched myself into misrule
As though the impulse was magnetic.
My tutors called me *energetic*-
That's how you say a boy's a fool,
I subsequently learned, if he
Is from a wealthy family.
My son will be my opposite:
A man of prudence, judgement, wit.
He'll pick a worthy cause to serve
And, in that purpose, never swerve.

And if my boy should be a girl,
Which he will not you understand,
The news would still be just as grand.
I'd stroke her wispy hair and twirl
My finger round a little curl,
While she demands my wedding band
By flexing her small, chubby hand.
All daughters are their father's pearl,
Virtue and chastity's quintessence
(Until they get to adolescence).
I've often said I want a boy,
But I'd be overcome with joy
To cultivate a fragile bud
Into the bloom of womanhood.

She'd grow into a gorgeous flower,
So feminine, so soft and fair,
That jealous matrons would all stare
And meanly wish her to the Tower
For making them seem tired and dour.
She'd float on beds of cushioned air
And young admirers everywhere
Would be completely in her power.
She'd be kind-hearted, true and wise,
Possessed of many quick replies
To put her suitors in their places.
The scattered wealth of female graces
Would come together as a whole
In one unblemished, cherished soul.

Dash it all! I cannot abide
This waiting any longer. Oh!
Why must the process be so slow?
Unless my mind is occupied,
My thoughts will soon begin to slide
Into scenarios of woe.
When will the little monkey show
Himself? Don't breathe!.. A knock outside!
At last! The news at last! And just
In time to save my wits. It must
Be Catherine's maid. Wipe off that grin,
You silly goose, and show her in.
We haven't got all day. Jump to it!

Maid enters.

Is it a boy? It is! I knew it!

MAID

No, it's a girl. I've only seen
Her for a moment. The physician
Suffered my presence on condition
That I remained behind a screen.
I wiped the little angel clean
And got a scathing admonition
Because I didn't ask permission.
I thought I'd had it but the Queen
Glanced playfully at me so, when
He'd gone, I picked her up again-
For just a moment, mind. She's such
A sweet, plump face. I went to touch
Her cheeks and then she tried to pull
My finger. Oh, she's beautiful.

THOMAS SEYMOUR, BARON OF SUDELEY

A girl! Ha ha! And clearly in
Good health! It was a lengthy birth,
To say the least, but it was worth
It. *Now*, you rascal, you may grin.
I wonder if there's ever been
Such hardship, ending in such mirth,
In all the ages of the Earth
As we have known. It makes the skin
Become all pimply, does it not?
Ah, maid! Good woman, I forgot
To ask about the Queen. She too,
I trust, is strong and healthy. You
Provided for her comfort, I
Suppose? My dear, what's wrong? Don't cry.

MAID

Oh God! I'm sorry! I'm concerned,
Lord Sudeley that the Queen's not well.
She asked me for some herbs to smell.
I fetched them but she tossed and turned
Regardless. Her whole body burned
As hot as coals dug out from hell
Itself. I quickly rushed to tell
The strict physician, but he'd learned
Already of her sickness. *She
Can wait*, he snarled, *until I'm free*.
At last he came. He'd brought a phial
With him. He huffed and shook it while
I smoothed Queen Catherine's sheets and said
A prayer. Oh, sir! She looked half-dead.

THOMAS SEYMOUR, BARON OF SUDELEY

Your mistress looked tired out, you mean?
Let us approach this sensibly,
Like adults. You've just said to me
That, when you wiped the baby clean
And thought you had done wrong, the Queen
Glanced playfully at you. So she
Was fine at that point, you'll agree?
I'm sure that, in your time, you've seen
More births than most. It's been a long,
Hard night. You have done nothing wrong
At all. You've done extremely well,
In fact. Try calmly now to tell
Me, did the Queen's physician give
Her some of his restorative?

MAID
I'm sorry, sir. I will stay calm.
The Queen's physician bent down low
Beside the bed and made as though
He rubbed a drop of that strange balm
Into Queen Catherine's open palm.
It wasn't much but, even so,
My mistress went as white as snow.
I said it's doing her more harm
Than good and asked him what it were
That he was rubbing into her.
He didn't answer me. He just
Rubbed more and more in and then cussed
Under his breath. Half-crazed with fear,
I left the chamber and ran here.

THOMAS SEYMOUR, BARON OF SUDELEY
He *cussed*? You mean to say he *swore*?
And, when he used his liniment,
Rubbing it in, your mistress went
All white? All pale? It didn't cure
Her? It just made her worse? And you're
Quite certain he did not relent.
The Queen's physician was hell-bent
On simply using more and more?—
You have been working like a slave
These past twelve hours. You likely crave
Some sleep. I think it would be best
For you to have a little rest.
We're all exhausted. Go and take
A nap. We'll talk more when you wake.

Maid exits.

175

GENTLEMAN-IN-WAITING
That was a nifty tune she played.
So much for sending her to bed,
I would have struck her off instead.
You ought to put her up for trade,
Procure yourself a newer maid.
When they grow old, they lose the thread.
Lord Sudeley! You have gone all red.
Surely to God you're not afraid
That what this hussy says is true?
Forget the maggot-brained old shrew.
A servant is in no position
To criticise the Queen's physician.
And she's a woman, after all.
She can't see sense. Her brain is small.

THOMAS SEYMOUR, BARON OF SUDELEY
If Catherine dies, then I'll die too,
Though in a far, far crueller way.
I'll die not once but every day,
When waking brings the news anew:
Your wife is dead, yes dead, it's true.
If Catherine goes to heaven, may
I quickly follow. You must pray
For me. I don't know what I'd do
If my wife dies. I don't know what
I'd do. I would go mad. I'd plot
The ruin of the state. I'd bring
My grief to bear on everything
And everyone. God, hear my plea:
Don't take my wife. Please, pray for me.

8: *A letter from Paget, written at his residence in Staffordshire, to Somerset in London.*

PAGET
Your Grace, I hope you will excuse
My recent self-imposed detention.
A note has brought to my attention
The spread of certain slanderous views
To the effect that I *abuse*,
Deform, *subvert*, and *wreck* convention.
It is this dissident's contention
That you, Lord Somerset, *refuse*
So much as to *engage your wit*
With anyone who does not sit
Within the *secret inner core*.
The note goes on. I could say more:
The Duke and Paget rule alone…
Their council bench is made a throne.

I cannot tell what evil wrought
A thing so manifestly blind.
A priest would say it was designed,
With every disobedient thought,
In that place where the devil taught
His angels to be of one mind.
The note is threateningly signed:
A councillor who offers nought.
It was delivered to my feet
While I was walking in the street,
As though it were an out-lawed text.
Needless to say, I felt perplexed.
I told the hooded wretch to stay,
But he'd discreetly slinked away.

Of course, I do not lift the lid
Upon this register of lies,
To make Your Grace's temper rise
Or frighten you, may God forbid,
But rather to show why I hid
Myself away from peeping spies
And other councillors' green eyes.
I love you as I ever did.
Your much-maligned friend simply meant
To mitigate the discontent
Which plagues the body politic
And makes the English nation sick.
When states, like little tots, grow ill,
One must administer a pill.

And yet I fear that I have failed.
Your recent letter was austere,
Bereft of that light-hearted cheer
Which courtly manners once entailed.
The jealous seem to have availed
Themselves of my brief sojourn here
To pour their bile into your ear.
Has this ambitious band prevailed
Against your honest, loyal friend?
I hoped and prayed that you would send
Some sign or hint of your concern,
A veiled appeal for my return.
Your letter told me nothing new.
I'm at a loss for what to do.

My messenger has brought me news
That Lady Somerset, your wife,
Augments this catalogue of strife.
Perhaps I stepped on her new shoes
And gave Her Ladyship a bruise.
If she had leisure and a knife,
I'm told she'd try to take my life.
The general concord of your views
Elicits words of admiration
From women all across the nation-
Not least from my wife, Lady Anne.
But you must know that every man,
Even the scholar, Sir John Cheke,
Has known Her Ladyship's critique.

I know that it is not your style
To quake and quail in trepidation
At the materialisation
Of this or that new test or trial.
Your Grace's way is to beguile
The danger of the situation
With seemingly remote deflation
And a forever-buoyant smile.
In certain quarters, this goes far
To make you rather popular.
A blasé disregard will not,
However, charm the irate Scot.
Nor will a wishy-washy stance
Assist us with regard to France.

When jeopardy approached too near,
And I unwarily withdrew
From court, I framed an overview
Of matters touching you most dear
In form and type as they appear
To me, which, if it pleases you
To spend some moments to look through,
Would greatly ease my mounting fear.
I wish that I could meet Your Grace
To solve these issues face to face.
A good discussion's always better
Than even the most skilful letter.
This survey represents a dip,
Alas, in our relationship.

Although a hasty compilation,
It will, at least, heal one small rift.
Your wife, I've been informed, was swift
To find another aberration
This recent Michaelmas vacation.
Paget forgot to send a gift,
Displaying the inherent thrift
Of members of my social station.
Consider, then, this overview
A gift from one who cares for you.
Consider it a glass which shows
The statesman how to primp his clothes.
Study yourself, adjust the fit,
And men will joy to see your wit…

When did the Scottish war commence?
As I am sure Your Grace will know,
It started sixteen months ago.
Now do we think it makes good sense
To go to all of this expense,
Given our progress is so slow?
We're up against a stubborn foe
Who brings the same intransigence
To every task he carries out,
From fishing day and night for trout,
Persisting as they all swim free,
To cutting lines into a tree
With nothing but a toothless saw
Until his fingers are red-raw.

He is a strangely forceful man,
This archetypal Scot of ours.
He toils away for hours and hours,
Appearing no less vital than
He seemed before his work began.
He braves the snow and icy showers
As though possessed of stoic powers.
His creed is centred on his clan.
He shares in pagan rituals,
Praying within a ring of skulls.
Although these modes are false and wrong,
They fix him, rouse him, make him strong.
His heresies defy God's law,
But they've sustained him in this war.

I've often heard you proudly boast
That *English* soldiers grow their hair
And occupy themselves in prayer;
On Sabbath days receive the Host
And kneel to praise the Holy Ghost.
But, to my bottomless despair,
This is a view I cannot share.
A blind devotion is the most
We can expect from such a rude,
Uncultivated multitude.
They do *believe*, of that I'm sure.
Though what's in flopping to the floor
If those beliefs are as diverse
As buttons in a beggar's purse?

Allegiance is a fitful thing,
And earnestness more fitful still.
Today you have your men's good-will.
They love their country and their king.
They puff their chests out and they sing
Their songs of mythic martial skill.
They're only too content to kill.
The change of Winter into Spring
Will keep them going for a while.
But hunger will soon steal their smile.
They'll grow to hate the war and not
Their outward enemy, the Scot.
The day their bellies start to hurt,
Our cheery soldiers will desert.

The English captain has compassion.
He'll see his soldiers have lost weight.
He'll question them when last they ate.
He'll note the size of each man's ration.
He'll mark their faces, gaunt and ashen,
Their withered limbs, their halting gait,
Their stooping backs, no longer straight.
He'll struggle to contain his passion.
He'll see the Scottish camped nearby
And try to stifle a long sigh.
He'll grow to think about the war
And wonder what we're fighting for.
He'll start to miss his loving wife
And come to curse his soldier's life.

So do you think we should remain
Within the wretched northern glade
Trying to force, or else persuade,
The Scottish to accept our reign?
Or should we prudently refrain
From prosecuting this crusade
Until the Treasury has made
Sufficient coin to try again?—
Or rather, should we terminate
The war and focus on the state?
If, after your astute correction
Of my apprentice-like dissection
Of such affairs you want my view,
I'll promptly render it to you.

Your independence is your vice.
It almost broke my heart to hear
The way Your Grace began to sneer
When Smith put forward his advice.
We, all of us, are on thin ice.
I can't ignore the awful fear
That civic strife is edging near.
If you surround yourself with mice,
And send your experts all away,
Your influence will soon decay.
Think back to what you had before
We spoke outside King Henry's door.
Now think what we'd go on to do
If I were reconciled with you.

Quicker than you can even blink,
I'd be packed up and on my way.
I would reach London in one day,
If only you dipped pen in ink
And told me what you truly think.
If only you, just once, could say
That my opinion still holds sway,
That we are standing on the brink,
That you are needful of your friend
To set this country on the mend,
And that you'll reconnect our bond,
Of course, Your Grace, I would respond.
There's precious little time to waste.
I urge you, call me back post-haste.

9: *At Syon House.*

ROYAL MESSENGER
I think I'll tarry in the street.
I do not want to go in there
With Somerset. I wouldn't dare
Upset His Grace. If I repeat
My awful message, he will beat
Me like a dog. He'll smash a chair
Over my head. The Duke won't care
Who I've been sent by. He will treat
You better. You're his servant. Go
And tell him. I will wait below.
He'd rather the news came from you.
I'm really just a stranger. Do
Me a good turn. We're at his door.
Don't think about it any more.

HOUSEHOLD SERVANT
I'm sorry but I must refuse.
You should go in. I spend my days
Polishing silver dinner trays
And buffing up His Grace's shoes.
I cannot break this dreadful news.
Not *I*. If I so much as raise
My eyes to meet my master's gaze,
I have been warned he will abuse
Me for it. If I were to *speak*
To him, I'd likely have to seek
Another job- that's *if* he let
Me live. The Duke of Somerset
Is a hard man, a *very* hard
Man. No, you've thrown in your last card.

ROYAL MESSENGER

Then I will raise the stakes. I'll pay
You one whole shilling- I mean two,
Two shillings. All you have to do
Is enter through the door and say
That I was forced to dash away
And that I have entrusted you
With an important message to
Deliver. Then you just convey
The message, showing due respect.
There is no need to genuflect
Or blow a trumpet: just report
How Sudeley prowled the royal court,
Saw the King's guard dog, fired a shot,
And was arrested on the spot.

HOUSEHOLD SERVANT

It's true that I don't have a head
For pounds and pence, but even I
Know that's a ruse. In times gone by,
Before the coinage all turned red
With copper base, I might've said
I'd do it- but not these days. Why
Should I? You couldn't even buy
A decent loaf of fresh-baked bread
With two of these new shillings. No,
I've told you: *you* will have to go.
You'll need your money for some new
Teeth after he has beaten you
For what his brother's done. He'll clout
You with such force, he'll smash them out.

ROYAL MESSENGER
If you won't help me, then get back
To working through your list of chores
Like an old housewife. Sweep these floors
As well, you rascal. They're pitch-black.
If your cruel master does attack
Me, mark my words, my hurts and sores
May be considered jointly yours.
You work it out, fool. Here's a smack
To give you some idea. And here's
Another. I will box your ears
As artfully as any prize-
Fighter. I promise you, your cries
Will spook the Tower ravens. On
My oath, they will. Now get you gone.

Exit Household Servant.

That common servant! I will knock
His block off... Hold a moment yet—
The villain's caused me to forget
My message. Calm yourself. Take stock.
Oh! What's the use? Unless the shock
Kills him, I'm through. My hands are wet.
A full-grown man near-drowned in sweat!
You coward! How my friends would mock
Me if they saw me standing here,
Out of my wits with mortal fear.
Why ever did you try to steal
The King, Lord Sudeley? Now I feel
Faint. Courage! Heed your own advice:
Make your report and don't think twice.

Royal Messenger enters into
Somerset's private quarters.

187

ROYAL MESSENGER

Lord Somerset, I have been sent
Here by the King upon a sad
Errand. You surely will be mad
But, as you have a kindly bent,
I know I'll face no punishment
For merely passing on the bad
News. Ever since I was a lad
I've done this job. My life's been spent
In service, first to Henry, now
To Edward. I am baffled how
This happened. That he came so near—
It's terrifying. To be clear,
The fault was in no sense my own.
I'm just a servant to the throne.

SOMERSET

A grand performance! Give me more!
On with the show without delay!
Bring the whole troupe in right away!
No servant would burst through my door.
You must be from an acting corps.
Well, well. Today's my lucky day.
I want to watch the entire play.
Am I to take it you're on tour?
Can I expect a tragedy?
It rather sounds like one to me.
A young boy must needs play the King.
I do so hope that he can sing.
And who's the man that *came so near*…
The villain as it would appear.

ROYAL MESSENGER
I only wish it were a show,
Your Grace. I pray you'll pardon me.
I truly didn't mean to be
So rude in bursting in. I know
I'm interrupting. Shall I go
On? Very well. His Majesty
Has strictly charged myself to see
You get the news at once. And so,
Sure in the knowledge that I'll not
Be blamed for someone else's plot,
Trusting Your Grace would never spill
An innocent man's blood, I will
Not keep you dangling on a string:
Your brother tried to snatch the King.

SOMERSET
Please give that to me once again.
I don't believe it. Did he fail?
Then is my brother now in jail?
Why did he do it? He's insane.
How could he even entertain
Thoughts of a plot? I should assail
The rascal for this gross betrayal.
I ought to personally chain
Him to the stocks. I've every reason
To tear him limb from limb. It's treason.
He has contrived to throw the state
Into confusion. I should hate
Him no less than the fiends which dwell
Within the inner rings of hell.

Why do I merely feel frustration?
It's like I've climbed a lofty peak
Only to find the view is bleak.
Many a lesser violation
Has set alight my indignation.
No man can say that I am weak.
Nor do I have a tender streak.
Perhaps the news wants maturation,
As with a cheese which must grow old
To gain its flavour from the mould.
He tried to steal the King away!
And is His Majesty okay?
Of course he must be, mustn't he?
King Edward sent you here to me.

ROYAL MESSENGER
The King is well. There's not a mark
Upon him. His escape was fated,
Your Grace. Some ladies were sedated,
But that is all. The King's remark,
Good job my dog began to bark!
Put them at ease. The guards related
To me that Sudeley must have waited
Patiently for it to come dark
In a small nook or cranny where
He guessed the servants wouldn't care
To look. However, he forgot
About the King's Great Dane and shot
It when it howled. The loud report
Rumbled like thunder round the court.

The King, of course, awoke. His face
And the silk blankets on his bed
Had been adorned with specks of red-
So too the walls. Within the space
Of a few seconds, a bronze mace
Came crashing down on Seymour's head.
He soon recovered and was led
Straight to the Tower in disgrace.
Although His Highness laughs and jokes,
His uncle's folly surely chokes
Him inwardly. I think the King
Now badly needs Your Grace to bring
Him manly comfort. Shall I say
That you will soon be on your way?

SOMERSET
I will be there within the hour.
Thank God my brother spent his shot
Upon a barking dog and not
The royal blossom, yet to flower.
This is what comes from chasing power.
It causes a man's brains to rot
Until he starts to scheme and plot.
The two young princes in the Tower
Are brought to mind by this foul deed.
To satisfy his wanton greed,
The princes' uncle had them slain
Before they had a chance to reign.
Today provides a parallel.
We're lucky that the King is well.

One day King Edward will stand tall.
The coming years will raise him higher
Than the cloud-skewering church spire.
But old ghosts prompt us to recall
That even giants are born small.
Before my nephew hits the sky, a
Base crew of scoundrels who desire
Those greater than themselves to fall
Will issue from the foggy gloom
To plot my tender nephew's doom.
I'll have to let myself be led
In the hard choice which lies ahead.
Enjoin His Highness to stay strong.
Tell him that I will not be long.

10: *At Syon House.*

SOMERSET
As it is sometimes the first mate
Who points the captain the right way,
I've called you to my side today.
I want to privately debate
The issue of my brother's fate.
I don't suppose that I need say
The utter heartache and dismay
My brother's crime against the state
Has caused me since I heard the news.
I'm glad, at least, that Edward views
The whole thing with a level head
And manages to sleep in bed.
His youthful spirit still flies free.
Alas, the burden falls on me.

Although my brother is a fool,
I am reluctant to torment
Him with barbaric punishment.
It's my belief that being cruel
Would quite unquestionably fuel
My brother's self-destructive bent,
Facilitating his descent.
He might be given to misrule
And prone to ill-considered acts;
He might have tried to form sly pacts
With men who've fallen from high places
And now don't dare to show their faces;
Indeed his soul may well be black;
But I am loth to use the rack.

However, I am not naïve.
The snag with being all humane
Is that he will offend again.
As a result, I don't believe
That I can offer a reprieve.
Given that torture is arcane,
Does any valid course remain?
I think my brother should receive
A penalty which fits his crime.
It may well be that some more time
In prison helps to sort him out.
I do not entertain a doubt
That he already finds it hell
Confined within his little cell.

I'm told he wakes from hour to hour.
When the guards offer him some meat,
He sobs and says he cannot eat.
Perhaps we ought to let him cower
A good while longer in the Tower-
Get more accustomed to his suite,
Plot all its sixty-four square feet.
His sentence through, I'll curb his power.
The privy council will demand
My brother forfeits his best land.
And, over our affairs at sea,
He will have no authority.
Also, I'll strip his castle bare.
Lord Warwick, does all this sound fair?

WARWICK
I actually feel it's too
Fair- that is if you would dispense
Justice to fit a man's offence.
I mean, I see your point of view.
But really, have you thought it through?
I'm quite surprised. I almost sense
That you are making his defence.
He has committed treason. You
Suggest we must decide on either
The Tower or the rack, but neither
Will satisfy the law- he had
A loaded pistol. He is mad-
That is to say, the man's deranged.
I thought you hated him. What's changed?

SOMERSET
I will endeavour to explain.
Events have placed us either side
Of the political divide.
That still holds true and I maintain
That he's ambitious, rash and vain.
Despite all this, when Catherine died
I thought of him and, yes, I cried.
I felt his grief. I shared his pain.
I know that he's committed treason
And I can't give you any reason
Why I would now protect his life,
Except that when he lost his wife—
Well, there's no need to say it twice.
I am in need of your advice.

WARWICK
I'll put it this way: When the war
Began, your brother stayed behind.
Not only was he disinclined
To help you, Paget's agents saw
Him with the disgraced Chancellor,
Telling the latter how unkind
It seemed that he had been confined
For breaking an invented law.
Still while we both were fighting in
Scotland, your brother sought to win
Royal approval for his bold
Designs and bribed the King with gold.
Then, taking care they were not seen,
Lord Sudeley wed the grieving Queen.

Suffice to say that when you'd gone,
Lord Sudeley soon set out his stall-
For we should not forget that all
This wrangling took place in one
Month. And your brother's carried on
His quest to bring about your fall
Ever since. Can Your Grace recall
Arundel saying Haddington
Had been attacked? What happened then?
He moved against you once again,
That's what, suggesting he'd got my
Support- of course, a total lie.
He hoped to drag poor Arundel
Into his little scheme as well.

My point is that you needn't feel
That you're the villain. You must trust
Me on that. Though it might disgust
You, when your brother chose to steal
The King away, he knew the deal.
I think he understands what must
Perforce now happen to him, just
As I think you do. Some men seal
Their own fate. That's the way it is.
You're not to blame. The fault is his.
Remember it's your brother who
Committed this grave crime- not you.
There's no-one who will shed a tear
For him. To me, the choice seems clear.

SOMERSET
I can't dispute a thing you've said.
He should be killed, but you forget
We're brothers. If we'd never met,
If it were someone else instead
Up for the chop, I'd have his head.
I'd say he shot the monarch's pet
Which thereby proves he posed a threat
To our dear King- and he'd be dead.
I know I'm now unpopular
Amongst the magnates, so how far
Will council back me if I choose
To let my brother live? Who'll use
My clemency against me? Who
Will murmur? Who will turn the screw?

WARWICK

They all will- that's apart from me.
I'd back you. I'm content to fight
Your cause regardless of how slight
The chances are. But you should be
Aware, the rest will want to see
Him killed. The magnates could still bite
You if your actions reunite
The council. Letting traitors free
Is apt to do just that. Your Grace
Would very likely have to face
A lot of angry opposition.
Those who you've lulled into submission
Will leave their country halls for town,
And they will try to bring you down.

Although the councillors berate
You over the long, drawn-out war,
Most of them have stayed loyal for
King Edward's sake. They tolerate
Your steely grip upon the state.
But if you now subvert the law,
That may well be the final straw.
It's possible they'd throw their weight
Behind a rival. As I've said,
Lord Sudeley is already dead.
Unfortunately, you can't save
A traitor. He has dug his grave
Through his own folly. It's a shame,
But you are not the one to blame.

SOMERSET

I don't suppose they can be bought?
You're sure that, if I made a stand,
They'd form into a tight-knit band?
Then it is worse than I had thought.
My harassed soldiers haven't fought
So bravely under my command
In such a barren, godless land
For me to let it come to nought.
You truly think I'd lose my power
If I preserved him in the Tower?—
If I just slightly bent the law,
They might rise up against my war?
Then is it Scotland or my brother?
Can I have one but not the other?

If time could somehow be reversed,
I would scrub out this tragic case,
Or drop another in his place.
Although my heart is fit to burst,
I have to put the nation first.
Some categories of disgrace
Must needs be met by death's embrace.
Unbiased logic has coerced
Me into making a hard choice.
I am now speaking with the voice
Of pure, disinterested reason:
Somebody has committed treason.
Regardless of the traitor's name,
Treason is treason all the same.

Because our lives are merely leased,
The condemned man cannot bemoan
The loss of that he does not own.
I will allow him one last feast.
I'll also let him see a priest.
No prayers, however, will atone
For his attempt against the throne.
Death by the axe is quick, at least.
I have arrived at my decision
Through a clear-sighted moral vision.
The only proper retribution
For such a crime is execution.
See that arrangements are soon made.
I thank you, Warwick, for your aid.

11: *A letter from Paget, written at his residence in Staffordshire, to Somerset in London.*

PAGET

Your Grace, I'm writing once again
Because I feel I have to try
To illustrate more clearly my
Opinions on the long campaign
In Scotland. It will be in vain,
Of course. I sometimes don't know why
I bother when you don't reply—
But stop my pen! I won't complain
This time. I have already burnt
Seven draft letters. If it weren't
So late, I'd burn one more. It's been
A trying day. I didn't mean
To start with such a haughty tone.
I know the fault is not your own.

I blame the jealous who conspire
To keep the two of us apart.
My colleagues' falseness makes me smart.
I never wanted to retire
To a soft life in Staffordshire.
I tell you with an open heart
That I would happily depart
For London if you so desire.
I used to be your foremost guide.
I'm wasted in the countryside.
I'd put the nation back on track
If you'd admit you need me back.
Or can't you say it, Somerset?
I fear not, much to my regret.

A weary message-bearer pressed
A note into my hand today
From Smith. The latter heard you say
That I'm as bad as all the rest.
If it's the case that you detest
Me, I'll remain a castaway
And leave the state in disarray.
Perhaps you spoke those words in jest?
Whatever, I won't bear a grudge.
You're usually a fair judge.
I think you know that, in the end,
I am your dearest, truest friend—
So many men have schemed and lied.
Maybe Smith too is now green-eyed.

I've heard your brother is now dead
As a result of his device.
Death seems to me a heavy price.
You didn't have to take his head.
You could have locked him up instead
And let him intrigue with the mice.
If you were acting on advice,
I am afraid you were misled,
As killing the poor, helpless fool
Made you appear extremely cruel.
As you're no doubt aware, the King
Thinks you have done a heinous thing,
As it's His Majesty's belief
That Sudeley couldn't think for grief.

The magnates whom I've spoken to
Are similarly full of ire.
There was no popular desire
To push his execution through.
I'm eager to discover who
Suggested this would raise you higher.
He is an evil, two-faced liar.
You rose to power with a coup
And you will likely fall by one,
Unless this fellow is soon gone.
The days when you could just ignore
The grumbling magnates are no more.
Therefore, in all you do, take care
That you are wise and true and fair.

I can't undo your brother's fate,
So there is no point looking back.
Although we are still wearing black,
We have to think about the state.
The Admiral owned much gold plate.
Send out a man you trust to pack
It all into a great, big sack,
Then sell it at the going rate—
I haven't lost my wits- not yet.
The Treasury is in huge debt.
And when a rich man's lips turn blue,
He's a good source of revenue.
I know this sounds a little cold,
But the Exchequer must have gold.

Official figures make it clear
That for each Scot our soldiers kill,
There's half a bag of charge to fill.
Given that powder's now so dear,
And union still nowhere near,
It won't be very long until
We're down to using pike and bill.
Our stores will quickly disappear.
When meat and drink's in short supply,
The men are told they must get by
On victuals they've scavenged for.
You say that's commonplace in war.
But powder can't be ground from rock
When armouries run out of stock.

Our men can't turn to face the sky
And chant together to invoke
The pagan gods of fire and smoke-
Although they have been known to try.
If they need powder, we must buy
It. But how can we if we're broke?
Should the state rob the honest folk
Responsible for our supply?
Is that your economic plan:
To make a slave of every man?
Perhaps you aim to build a nation
Where no-one gets remuneration
For labouring from day to day:
An entire country on no pay.

My servants still in London say
That there have been, on average, more
Than ten men knocking on my door-
Not every week, but every day-
In the few months I've been away.
They are all desperately poor.
They come to see if there's a chore
That they can carry out for pay.
Each of them has a tale of woe,
But hardly any of them know
The truth of why they're destitute.
When they come up to make their suit,
I wonder quite how many think
That war has brought them to the brink?

While they curse men of high renown,
There hasn't been a single case
When someone's railed against Your Grace.
The day you last rode out round town,
Dressed up in your fine scarlet gown,
One beggar stopped his plea to race
Outside and glimpse your noble face.
My greedy lord has dragged me down,
But not the Duke of Somerset.
He hasn't put a foot wrong yet.
Let him keep up his war, says I.
Those heathen Scots deserve to die.
This man supports the war in full.
My servants say he's typical.

Most supplicants are quick to mention
That everything you do is great.
But there's no cause to celebrate.
The other, uglier dimension
To all this is a new class-tension.
Allow me to explain. Of late,
Squires have been living in a state
Of almost constant apprehension.
When tenants can't afford their leases
And the poor-rich divide increases,
The poor will find the rich to blame.
Whilst this has always been the same,
That beggar who rushed out to see
You chained his landlord to a tree.

But what does such a trifle show?
And isn't it a bit absurd
And off the point that I've referred
To it at all? Perhaps. Although,
Let's now think back. Twelve months ago,
Were passions adequately stirred
For this event to have occurred?
Or did the common people grow
Contemptuous and somehow surer
As they were all becoming poorer?
That beggar's not-so-petty crime
Is singularly of our time.
And it's as nothing next to what
Is slowing cooking in the pot.

That beggar's type will raise the call.
And men who haven't got a bean
Are very easily made mean.
I've made provision for a wall
To be put up around my hall.
It is ostensibly a screen
To shade my lawns and keep them green—
It's four feet thick and eight feet tall.
That ought to give you some idea
Of what I think is drawing near.
Forget the conflict in the glen.
It won't be Scots but gentlemen,
Squires, men of leisure, knights and lords
Who'll soon be slain by English swords.

The poor will shortly make a claim
On land and money and rich wares
And all that isn't rightly theirs.
They'll put great manors to the flame,
Burning them to an empty frame.
They will catch landlords unawares,
And drag them to their secret lairs-
And they will do it in your name.
The common people cannot see
That you're their rightful enemy.
It is ironic: they adore
The very man who's made them poor.
I will now put my pen away.
I've written plenty for today.

I'll sleep a restless sleep tonight.
Internal strife will be the theme
Of many an unpleasant dream.
I'd gladly spurn the hour and write
Till morning in the candlelight.
I love to see the wet ink gleam,
Appearing like a winding stream.
However, it will strain my sight.
And it is painful to reflect
On errors which I could correct
If you would let yourself be taught.
I'll leave you with this final thought:
Is it through wisdom or through pride
That you are blanking your best guide?

12: *At Warwick's residence, Dudley Castle, situated in the West Midlands.*

WARWICK

Even in death he had no luck.
Poor, poor Sir Thomas. As they led
Him to the wooden block, I said
A heart-felt prayer. His body shook
So much, the executioner took
Two botched attempts to get his head
Off. I could tell he wasn't dead
After the first. I had to look
Away. I'm not a stranger to
The sight of bloodshed, but to view
The execution of a friend-
I only wanted it to end.
It almost made me sick. The crowd-
Those rotten villains- cheered aloud.

ARUNDEL

Those beasts on stage were also mean.
To see that burly man display
My colleague's head in that lewd way-
I found the whole thing quite obscene.
It truly was a gruesome scene.
I had to force myself to stay
And somehow keep my rage at bay.
If Sudeley hadn't lost the Queen,
We would be talking with him now.
It puts a sweat upon my brow
To think that if that damned physician
Had comprehended her condition-
Well, it is done. Did you attend,
My Lord Wriothesley, in the end?

WRIOTHESLEY
I stood there rooted to the spot
As that great axe came crashing down,
Spilling warm blood upon my gown.
Lord Sudeley was an idiot
To dream up such a silly plot.
Perhaps he planned to go round town
Wearing King Edward's golden crown.
I do not think he would have shot
His much beloved nephew, though.
I would imagine you both know
Far more about this case than me.
However, I can clearly see
The Lord Protector's hand in this.
If I may briefly reminisce…

A few days after Henry died,
I made a visit to His Grace.
I told the devil to his face
That I would never take his side.
Won't you, indeed? the Duke replied,
Then I will see to your disgrace.
I'll cage you up in Ely Place.
And you he snarled *will never ride*
Through London's ancient streets again.
He even threatened to detain
Me as a traitor in the Tower
As his first act on taking power.
My own rough treatment clearly shows
How he behaves towards his foes.

WARWICK
Indeed, my lord. I sympathise
With you. He's rude to Arundel
And me, but you have gone through hell
Because of him. I can't disguise
The fact that I for one despise
Lord Somerset. I tried to tell
Him to keep Sudeley in his cell.
Until the councillors advise
You otherwise, I begged him, *do*
Not execute your brother. You
Must wait, Your Grace, I pleaded, *for*
Us to discourse upon the law
A little and decide his fate.
Alas! The scoundrel didn't wait.

ARUNDEL
Be comforted. You tried your best.
Though Sudeley never was my friend,
I'm also sad he met his end.
It's natural to feel distressed
For a short while and beat one's breast.
However, one must not expend
Warm tears on things one cannot mend.
In some ways, Sudeley has been blessed.
By happy accident of birth,
He never had to plough the earth.
The Baron always had good health,
And he enjoyed both rank and wealth.
After a mostly happy life,
He is now once more with his wife.

As for the Duke of Somerset,
The man who governs on his own,
Thinking he sits upon the throne;
The man who trapped us in his net
Where we remain entangled yet;
He's once again quite clearly shown
That tyrants' hearts are made of stone.
He saw his brother as a threat.
Therefore the Duke removed his head-
Despite the fact Lord Warwick pled
With him to give the council time
To ponder over Sudeley's crime.
I know that I'll find no rebuke
In saying I too hate the Duke.

WRIOTHESLEY
I don't particularly mind
The executing of a fool—
Well, that is as a general rule.
But as I still feel much maligned
For the Duke's having me confined
Like a young boy found skipping school,
I'll also say that it was cruel.
Thus our opinions are aligned.
His Grace's faults have added up.
The Duke has drained his goodwill cup.
He has pursued a costly war
And he has undermined the law,
Going against your sound advice.
So what, my lords, will be his price?

WARWICK

Be careful, my old friend. We've got
To watch ourselves. Whilst I care nought
For my life, this bold line of thought
Will lead us all toward a plot.
And once we've started, we cannot
Go back. The way ahead is fraught
With danger. Somerset has fought-
Off many foes. He's faced a lot
Of hardy dissidents and he
Is still on top. What chance do we
Stand of defeating him? Three cowed
Nobles against a tyrant, proud
And powerful? I must confess,
I think it's hopeless— that's unless…

ARUNDEL

My Lord, you keep us in suspense.
When Sudeley was so meanly killed,
I felt my very soul was chilled.
I'm not for sitting on the fence.
I'll back you if your plan makes sense.
You'll find me upright and strong-willed.
My pledge, once made, will be fulfilled.
I'm not the sort who makes pretence
Of being ready for a fight
Only to flee once out of sight.
My loyalty won't wane through terror
Because I know we're not in error.
Our duty is towards the King,
And we are doing the right thing.

WARWICK
We are, my lord. I will lay bare
My plan: Most common folk resent
Their landlords racking up the rent.
Am I correct? So there's a fair
Chance that revolts will shortly flare
Up. Now, to combat this dissent,
It's likely soldiers will be sent
To all the shires and hamlets where
The trouble is. But where will these
Troops come from? They don't grow on trees.
Will Somerset withdraw his men
From their positions in the glen
To fight the English rebels, or
Will he prioritise his war?

The latter seems more likely to
Me. You may disagree, but I'd
Say that it all comes down to pride.
Of course, he might withdraw a few
Soldiers, but it's the likes of you
And me, the nobles, who'll provide
The troops he needs to stem the tide
Of rebels. It is our men who
Lord Somerset will count upon.
His skeletons at Haddington
Will almost certainly stay out
Of it. I'd say there's little doubt
Our forces will be mobilised-
And once the serfs have been chastised…

WRIOTHESLEY
…We'll have an army in the field!
A clever scheme indeed, my lord.
England will churn in disaccord.
If Somerset declines to yield,
His fate will surely then be sealed
By the swift down-stroke of a sword.
So will the chroniclers record
The way old wounds were justly healed
In summer, Fifteen Forty-Nine.
I think Lord Warwick's plan is fine.
In fact, I think we cannot fail.
You have my word: I won't turn tail.
All you need do is tell me when,
And I'll put out four thousand men.

ARUNDEL
That is a bit too steep for me.
You did say you will put out four?
And people say that you are poor!
At present, I will only be
Able to manage two or three.
I'm sorry I can't give you more,
But that still makes a good-sized corps.
Like my rich colleague, I agree
Your plan is very well thought-out.
And I do not have any doubt
That God will put events in place
To help us dispossess His Grace.
All that is left for me to say
Is I'll be ready, come the day.

WARWICK
I thank you both. I see we trust
Each other. Good. Before I take
My leave of you, I'd like to make
This known: We're acting not through lust
For power, but because we must.
We have no choice. We have to break
The Duke's control for England's sake.
Therefore, our enterprise is just.
Goodbye, my friends. For now, we'll wait.
Given the miserable state
The country's in, with people praying
For change, I think I'm right in saying
It won't be long until commotion-
Time, when we'll put our plans in motion.

13: *A letter from Paget, written at his residence in Staffordshire, to Somerset in London.*

PAGET
Your Grace, how many diverse ways
Have I churned out the same old tale?
The message must, by now, be stale.
Like blackened clouds, a deep malaise
Bears down upon my lonely days.
Will common sense at last prevail,
Or am I sadly doomed to fail?
If there are yet some cheery rays
Still dimly shining through the trees,
These are the fading memories
Of all the joyful times we've shared,
Reminding me that, once, you cared.
The hope you'll love your friend again
Is the one thing that keeps me sane.

When I was only ten years old,
I can recall that I once snuck
Into a library for a book.
I always did as I was told,
But this day I was feeling bold
And rather keen to try my luck.
I'd brought along a crude, wire hook
Which I looped through the corner fold
Of an impressive-looking tome.
I pulled it down and ran off home,
Thinking myself extremely clever.
I don't suppose that I will ever
Forget the meaning in those pages.
Some lessons seem to span the ages.

The story was the fall of Troy.
I think I could still quote you each
And every god and hero's speech.
I truly loved it as a boy.
I shared my countrymen's great joy
As the Greek vessels left our beach.
Our walls had proved too hard to breach.
But was the wooden horse a ploy?
Cassandra said it should be burned.
When, just five pages on, I learned
The gift was an audacious trick,
I thought I'd better change sides quick-
I was, I should repeat, just ten.
But something struck me even then:

The reason that the Greek device
Worked out was due to Priam's pride.
His daughter, poor Cassandra, tried
To give the Trojan King advice,
But Priam had the tyrant's vice.
Cassandra's visions were denied,
And she was cruelly cast aside.
Cassandra begs King Priam thrice
To burn the wooden horse to ashes.
But then a mighty war-cry crashes
Around King Priam's vaulted halls.
The Greeks have entered and Troy falls.
The city sacked; King Priam killed;
Cassandra's prophecy fulfilled.

Now let's consider your decision
To shun my warnings in this light,
And question if your choice was right.
Your prophet also had a vision,
Which Your Grace greeted with derision.
There are no Greeks you'll have to fight-
Though you have enemies alright.
So can't we point to an elision
Between the mythic and the real?
Is not Cassandra's vain appeal
In essence similar to mine?
And can't we say, when you decline
To heed my prophecies, that you
Are acting quite like Priam too?

I wonder if Your Grace has read
The same account of when Troy fell.
If you have not, it's just as well.
It says there were so many dead,
The city streets were all stained red.
It truly was a scene from hell.
The Greeks left Troy an empty shell.
I harbour a great sense of dread
That such a fierce and dire eruption
Of violence, hatred and destruction
Is not confined to legend's rhymes,
And may occur in modern times.
Indeed, reports are coming through
That my worst nightmares have come true.

Much to my very deep regret,
It seems the lawless Norfolk shires
Have moved against their local squires.
Do not believe them, Somerset,
When they profess they pose no threat.
Their actions prove them to be liars.
They all have sinister desires,
None more so than their leader, Kett:
A gentleman who joined their band
In order to protect his land,
And soon took on a vicious role.
So long as he is in control,
No squire is safe for miles around
And evil mischief will abound.

Kett hunts down gentlemen like deer.
If they refuse his cruel demand
To give the peasants all their land,
The rebels sound an awful cheer
And prick their captives with a spear.
The helpless squires must then withstand
The torment of a cattle-brand,
Until they faint through pain or fear.
Kett might contend he's fighting greed
But what will this false justice breed,
Save generations of ill will?
He finds rebellion a thrill.
Only base reasons motivate him.
All wealthy men in Norfolk hate him.

Whilst Kett's revolt is localised,
His crimes are copied nationwide.
The Rule of Law is on the slide.
Squires are so thoroughly despised,
They're lucky if they're not chastised.
Some gentlemen attempt to hide
In places where they can't be spied.
One landlord fled abroad disguised
As a bedraggled stable boy
Before his tenants could destroy
His modest farmstead while he slept.
A vassal tried to intercept
This poor man's passage the next day.
Thanks be to God, he got away.

Although the knaves are led by spite,
Not all are singing the same song.
The heretics complain it's wrong
To paint a House of God in white.
This faction says it isn't right
For priests to use our native tongue.
In Cornwall, there exists a throng
Of papists itching for a fight.
It's difficult to comprehend:
They're so determined to defend
Their idol-venerating ways,
That they would set a church ablaze—
But harder still to understand
Is why you haven't made a stand.

When you put out your proclamation
Forgiving those who have rebelled,
Kett's numbers actually swelled.
They took it as an intimation
That you support their demonstration.
If you would see these tumults quelled,
I think, at this point, you're compelled
To make a stronger publication,
In which it should be clearly stated
That they will not be tolerated.
Upbraid the fools for how they bring
Great woe to you and to the King.
So long as they think you're their friend,
This present strife will never end.

When peaceful means have run their course,
If peasants still cause untold harms,
Making their landlords leave their farms,
You surely need not feel remorse
Should you decide on using force.
Don't delay sounding the alarms
To signal to your men of arms.
I'm certain council will endorse
A plan to put them in their places.
There have been far too many cases
Of violent discord for soft words.
When dealing with unruly herds,
It's no good saying they're forgiven.
They're merely cattle to be driven.

Though this might seem self-evident,
I worry that you don't agree.
I often fear you cannot see,
One can't stamp down upon dissent
By asking rebels to repent.
Before you let them all run free,
Remember what you promised me
When Henry's life was almost spent
And we embraced outside his door.
Remember what Your Grace then swore
On that cold, dark and misty night,
When our late monarch had to fight
For every laboured, wheezing breath
In an attempt to stave off death.

The moment the King's life-blood chilled,
I handed you the English nation.
Alas, Your Grace's obligation
To me is sadly unfulfilled.
You praised me, saying I was skilled
At statecraft in your estimation,
And well-equipped for my vocation.
You said together we would build
A thriving milk and honey state.
It is upsetting to relate
How lucky and how glad I felt
With this new hand that I'd been dealt.
I'm running out of paper— Send
For me, Your Grace. I'm still your friend.

14: *In the newly built wing of Somerset House.*

SOMERSET
Paget, this ludicrous divide
Between us has to be unbuilt.
Whilst a good deal of ink's been spilt,
Little's been said by either side.
Though I'm a martyr to my pride,
I think we have to share the guilt—
All friendships are a patchwork quilt:
We'll drift apart and we'll collide;
We will know happiness and strife,
And all the ups and downs of life.
I felt abandoned when you'd gone.
But now you're back, we must move on.
I'm not too arrogant to say
I'm sorry that you went away.

PAGET
I am so glad we're reconciled.
When we're together, we are strong.
Although you moderate your tongue,
I can imagine you are riled
At my behaving like a child.
I will admit that I was wrong
To keep from London for so long.
Before I say that fate has smiled
Upon us hapless souls at last
And that our woe is in the past,
Please tell me what I need to hear:
Say there's no longer cause to fear
The safety of King Edward's crown.
Please say you've put the rebels down.

SOMERSET

You've not been told? I thought you knew.
You will be pleasantly surprised.
They have been thoroughly chastised.
It pained me but I saw it through—
Believe me, Paget, it is true.
I put them down as you advised.
My soldiers marched unadvertised
Up to Kett's rebel camp and slew
Around three thousand of the swine—
I talk as if the troops were mine.
They were Lord Warwick's men, in fact.
I can't take credit for the act.
He hasn't charged the Treasury.
He kindly raised a force for free.

It is a shame in one respect.
In the demands Kett's rebels sent,
They showed they had a fair intent.
They were quite possibly correct
That landlords' powers should be checked.
When no-one can afford the rent,
There's little option save dissent.
You know that they did not direct
Their wrath against His Majesty?
And they were most polite to me.
Maybe it's that which held me back.
They seemed too loyal to attack.
But when they misconstrued my pardon,
I knew my methods had to harden.

I put the papists down as well,
And in so doing foiled their plot
To march on London. I am not
Sure quite how many of them fell.
My captains say it's hard to tell
Precisely, but it was a lot.
Of course, their leaders will be shot.
If they desire to go to hell,
I will oblige them. Unlike Kett's
Rebels, the papists dealt in threats-
Though they are to be thanked for that.
It's easier to kill a rat
Than an unmanageable yet
Essentially devoted pet.

As for the country as a whole,
Although some purging still awaits,
We are no longer in dire straits.
I've reasserted my control.
Squires are now free once more to stroll
Around their beautiful estates.
They will look back and praise the Fates
Their heads weren't put upon a pole
In a barbarian display
The time the peasantry held sway.
We have stamped down upon dissent.
The English gentry are content
That I preserved them in the end-
But it is you they should commend.

When law and order fell apart,
You, my dear friend, did all you could
To make things better. Common blood
Can travel through a noble heart.
Now, when the tranquil sunbeams start
To dry and crack the fields of mud,
The flower of new peace will bud.
The peasant will load up his cart
And wheel it through the squire's barn door
The way he's always done before.
And if there's some injustice there
And folk still say it isn't fair,
I am afraid that such is life.
We can't be having civic strife.

PAGET
The poor still suffer but I own,
It's through sheer joy my cheeks are wet.
The rebels posed a grievous threat.
All of them were against the throne.
Charm and politeness can't atone
For what they've done. I don't regret
The deaths of those who followed Kett.
And backward papists who bemoan
The spreading of reformed belief
Aren't worthy objects of our grief.
Great happiness is surging through me.
You actually listened to me!
I'm so elated, I could sing.
There is, however, one more thing:

Unless by happy chance he died
Whilst prosecuting his attack,
That devil, Warwick, must be back.
In which dark corner does he hide,
This sly deceiver, this false guide?
I'd like to put him on the rack
And stretch him till his bones all crack
For the cruel way the villain lied,
Misrepresenting council's views
To lay the groundwork for some ruse.
I'll tear the rascal limb from limb.
I have discovered it was him,
This reveller in others strife,
Who made you take your brother's life…

…Your Grace, please tell me that you read
The recent letter which I sent
Touching upon that sad event.
I told you that you were misled:
Your brother could have kept his head.
I questioned if your guide was bent
On shrewdly plotting your descent.
I'm certain that I clearly said
It was an outright, blatant lie
That council wanted him to die.
Don't tell me this is news to you.
You do know Warwick is untrue?
I'll hasten to his residence.
I hope he has a good defence.

SOMERSET

I will come with you. I know where
The villain lives. I didn't read
Your letter. What a foul misdeed.
The scoundrel! I was not aware
That council felt that way. How dare
He lie to me... Oh God! I need
A jug of wine or beer or mead,
Or anything— He won't be there,
The rascal! Paget, Warwick's still
Out in the country. I feel ill.
I must sit down. I asked him when
He's going to disband his men.
He hasn't given his reply,
And now I know the reason why.

He's going to attempt to seize
Power. He's planned an evil coup.
And God knows he will see it through
Unless we think of something. He's
A subtle Alcibiades
For our own time. It's worse than you
Supposed. Whatever will we do?
Fight him? What with? We can't appease
Him, that's for sure. No wonder he
Declined to charge the Treasury.
The spectre of a civil war
Was just what he'd been waiting for.
These riots gave him all he needed
To raise an army unimpeded.

Now's when you say I have inferred
Too much. Correct me. I'm not clever
Like you are. Tell me that you've never,
In all your time in office, heard
Such nonsense. Tell me it's absurd.
Say that no councillor would ever,
Not even in their dreams, endeavour
To topple me. We'll soon get word
That he has broken up his force
And sent his soldiers home. Of course
We will. It stands to reason. Why
Why, Paget, would Lord Warwick try
To challenge my Protectorate?
Would he bring ruin to the state?

PAGET
Alas! He would, Your Grace. I fear
We're in deep trouble. He's controlled
Your every motion. Let me hold
You. It is all becoming clear.
He had to make Your Grace appear
Tyrannical, and so he told
You with feigned mournfulness his bold
Lie. *You have got to be severe.*
The magnates want your brother dead.
You must cut off the traitor's head.
He had to make the lords detest
You so that, when the great unrest
Began and he could make his move,
He would be certain they'd approve.

SOMERSET

You mean they're all against me? No!
You're overthinking things. Let's pause
A moment. They have no real cause
To get behind him. You don't know
That he has all the lords in tow.
I will accept I've many flaws,
But I uphold my country's laws
And punish those who don't. They owe
Me thanks. I have just pacified
The entire English countryside.
I think that even you'd admit
That's an achievement, isn't it?
Gather your wits. We're both afraid,
But this is Warwick's lone crusade.

PAGET

It may be so. I hope and pray
He acts alone. My judgment might
Be taking shape more out of fright
Than neutral reason. Either way,
It is too dangerous to stay
In London even one more night.
Whether or not Your Grace is right,
Both of us must depart today
For our own safety. But before
We leave, it's crucial you implore
The King with all your heart to come
With us. And we should scatter some
Handbills to get the people on
Our side. Go now. We'll meet anon.

15: *In a small cell at Windsor Castle.*

KING EDWARD VI
…And why exactly do we dwell,
The three of us, in this cramped space?
Whatever trouble's taking place
Outside the confines of our cell,
I pray that, as your King, you'll tell
Me. I am very scared, Your Grace.
You turn to me a smiling face,
But I am sure that all's not well.
Something is wrong. I did not broach
The subject in your speeding coach
Because your eyes shot raging fire.
Now we've arrived, I do require
An explanation, uncle. Please,
One of you, put me at my ease.

SOMERSET
Your Majesty has got to trust
Me. I am deeply sorry to
Have frightened you. I know that you
Were understandably nonplussed
When my attendants swiftly thrust
You in my coach, but all I do
Is out of love. We must get through
This trial together, and we must
Contain our fear. Your Majesty
Has often said you want to be
A soldier when you're fully grown.
Those who are fighting don't bemoan
The cramped conditions. They behave
Like adults. They are strong and brave.

KING EDWARD VI
My heart, in former times, was set
On someday leading war-like men,
But I've matured a lot since then.
I asked a question, Somerset.
I haven't heard your answer yet.
I will inquire of you again:
Why am I trapped inside this pen?
I have been trying to forget
The awful thing which you have done.
I think I'd just about begun
To put that tragedy behind me,
But now, dear uncle, you've confined me,
I see my other uncle's head,
And I'm reminded why he's dead.

PAGET
Your Majesty is much confused,
And there I own the fault is mine.
It's not our meaning to confine
You. If you ask to be excused,
Of course, you wouldn't be refused.
Here, let me take your gown. Recline
Upon this pillow. Drink some wine.
You mustn't think yourself misused.
Your loving uncle brings you here
Because we have good cause to fear
That you're no longer safe at court.

Enter Messenger

Ah! Envoy, hand me your report.
Your coming is a great relief.
Is there no more than this one leaf?

SOMERSET
…Well, Paget? You've a face like stone.
Don't bother reading it all through.
Such bile will tell us nothing new.
The Duke rules England on his own;
He doesn't listen: Moan, moan, moan.
Skip past the empty prattle to
The signatories. Tell me who
They are. Does Warwick act alone?
That's what we really need to know.
For God's sake, hurry! Are you so
Leisurely all the time or just
When urgency is called for? Must
You study every single line?
Oh, damn you, then. I need some wine.

PAGET
You cannot damn a man to hell,
Your Grace, if he's already there.
Here's what you wish to know. Prepare
Yourself. It's signed by Arundel
And the ex-chancellor, as well
As Warwick. *We three lords declare*
The Duke's arrest…You must repair
To London now. We can compel
Your coming hither, have no doubt…
It is because you shut us out;
It's as you ruined England for
The sake of your beloved war;
It's as your manner's rude and curt,
And you have treated us like dirt—

SOMERSET

Enough, for heaven's sake! Enough,
Paget. The villains say they will
Arrest me? Never! Fetch a quill.
Give me some paper. They talk tough,
But I am made of sterner stuff
Than they've accounted for. I'm still
The Lord Protector and, until
They graduate from words- mere fluff
And schoolboy threats- and fight with me
And either hang me from a tree
Or slay me with a sword or brain
Me with a club, I will remain
This nation's ruler. Paget, ink!
I'll tell the devils what I think.

KING EDWARD VI

You'll leave the ink and bring my gown.
Lord Warwick's envoy will report
The Duke does not have my support.
I am the one who wears the crown.

Exit Messenger

I say we're going back to town.
You should have left me at my court.
Do you consider it a sport,
Turning my country up-side down?
I am the ruler of this nation.
I say there'll be no confrontation.
Too many men have died of late.
My subjects want a peaceful state—
You needn't fill your blasted cup!
I'm telling you, my mind's made up.

SOMERSET
I haven't filled this cup for me.
You are confused, as Paget said.
This wine will dull your sense of dread.
England needs concord, I agree.
But nephew, you must try to see,
If we go back they'll take my head,
Then both your uncles will be dead.
You do not know these men as we
Do. Ask me why my brother died.
That scoundrel, Warwick, was my guide.
He forced my hand. He told the lie
That council wanted him to die.
It was all Warwick's cruel design-
Not mine, Your Majesty. Not mine.

KING EDWARD VI
That doesn't change a single thing.
A person who holds justice dear
Would spurn the master puppeteer,
Not merely dangle on his string.
Now listen to me: I'm the King.
I'm not confused. My mind is clear.
I've told you we are leaving here
For London- Uncle, you can't cling
On to your tattered rags of power.
You should go meekly to the Tower.
It would be ill-advised to fight.
Paget will tell you I am right.
If you indulge in civic strife,
They surely will not spare your life.

PAGET

To take up arms with sword and shield
In an adventuresome last stand
Would be to turn this wounded land
Once more into a battle-field.
I also think Your Grace should yield.
The fact is you are undermanned.
Lord Warwick has the upper hand.
Oppose him and your fate is sealed,
His Majesty is quite correct.
But keep the peace and I suspect
Your story hasn't reached an end.
I'll always be your faithful friend.
Submit to him and I will strive,
I swear, to keep Your Grace alive.

SOMERSET

I see. At least I know now where
I stand. It's clear you've thrown your lot
In with Lord Warwick. It is not
The moral choice; it is not fair;
It's not what I deserve. But there
It is. You both support his plot.
I will be killed or left to rot
In jail and neither of you care—
Peace, nephew, Paget. I don't blame
You for it. I have played the game
Quite well. I knew that it would cost
Me if, or rather when, I lost.
It just remains to wait and see
Exactly what the cost will be.

If I should leave you, death will find
Me unconcerned. For many men,
Death seems a far-off thing and then
It pounces on them from behind.
For others, death's still more unkind.
It spreads its office over ten
Or fifteen years and only when
The body's broken and the mind
Is absent does it finish what
It started. I, thank God, will not
Suffer. There will be no decline.
I'll pour myself some good red wine
And I'll go out a proper way,
Able to toast my final day.

And if I am allowed to know
A little more of life, I'll try
To be content. I will not cry
About what's happened for, although
I'll be in jail, I will outgrow
My dank and dingy chamber. I
Will think I'm floating in the sky,
Or chatting with the folk below
My window. I will read all day,
And long-dead poets will convey
Exquisite thoughts to me and me
Alone. In truth, I will be free.
What if my body is confined?
Nobody can lock up my mind.

Well, that is all I have to say.
I don't suppose I can complain.
Your Majesty, I won't detain
You any longer. We won't stay
At Windsor. Let's be on our way.
I fear we will get wet again.
It looks as though it wants to rain.
It's been a miserable day.
It is October, though. July
And August were both very dry.
It's said that too much sun is bad
For crops. The farmers will be glad
Of a brief spell of dreary weather.
Come, Paget, we will leave together.

THE END

Epilogue

After the coup d'état in October 1549, Somerset was imprisoned in the Tower of London. His protectorate was dissolved.

In the privy council, a power struggle between the co-conspirators, Warwick and Wriothesley ensued. Aided by those councillors who were conservative in their religious beliefs, Wriothesley attempted to remove his new rival by claiming Warwick's complicity in Somerset's crimes. Warned of the imminent danger, Warwick made an attempt to win the council to his side. Warwick told the magnates that Wriothesley did 'seek his [Somerset's] bloude and he that seekethe his bloude woulde have myne also'.

The privy councillors gave Warwick their support. In January 1550, Wriothesley and also Arundel were placed under house arrest. The following month, Warwick became lord president of the privy council. In July of the same year, Wriothesley died. According to the churchman, John Ponet, 'fearing least he should come to some open shamefull ende, he either poisoned himself, or pyned awaye for thought'.

After Warwick had successfully dealt with his main rival, he felt secure enough to sanction Somerset's release from the Tower of London. After six weeks spent under house arrest, Somerset dined with the King on 8 April. He was readmitted to council two days later.

There is some evidence of a reconciliation between the two men, as in June Somerset's eldest daughter married Warwick's eldest son. However, Somerset was critical of Warwick's abandonment of his Scottish policy. It is also possible that Somerset's apparent idealism in social policy (as seen, for instance, by his pardoning the rebels in summer 1549) clashed with Warwick's more pragmatic and repressive stance towards the commons. In addition, Somerset remained ambitious. These factors prevented any long-term friendship between the pair.

In early 1551, rumours spread that Somerset desired the restoration of his former powers. It is possible that, by the summer, Somerset realised his hopes would not come to pass. Nevertheless, Warwick (who had been promoted to duke of Northumberland) chose to act on the allegation that Somerset planned to invite him to a banquet and cut off his head. On 16 October, Somerset was once again sent to the Tower, but this time on a charge of treason.

Somerset was tried by his peers in December 1551. He conducted his own defence and was acquitted of the charge of treason. But he was found guilty of the felony of raising a power of the commons on purpose to riot. The council's order to London householders to ensure the good behaviour of their apprentices during the trial attests to Somerset's continued popularity amongst the commons.

Though cleared of treason, Somerset's conviction of a felony provided sufficient grounds for Warwick to have his old rival executed. On the day of the execution, 22 January 1552, householders were told to stay indoors until 10a.m. Even so, a large crowd gathered on Tower Hill. A rumour that the Duke was going to be spared excited the crowd. The rumour proved to be false and Somerset was beheaded.

Warwick's ascendency was short-lived. On 6 July 1553, King Edward VI died. After failing to divert the succession from Mary Tudor, Warwick was tried for treason. He was executed on 22 August.

Through all the twists and turns and political manoeuvrings of the four years following the dissolution of the Somerset protectorate, Paget remained the clever, neutral and moderate statesman.

However, Warwick was keen to implicate Paget in the plot that Somerset stood accused of. Paget suffered a spell in the Tower of London, heavy fines and the stripping of his various offices.

During Mary's reign, he was restored to the privy council and, despite frequent bouts of ill health, Paget continued to serve some diplomatic function at the start of Elizabeth's reign. He died of natural causes in 1563.

Printed in Great Britain
by Amazon.co.uk, Ltd.,
Marston Gate.